COLWYN BAY
FOLK

COLWYN BAY FOLK

GRAHAM ROBERTS

AMBERLEY

For the memory of the voice of my father, Alan,
that still reverberates in my mind.

First published 2013

Amberley Publishing
The Hill, Stroud
Gloucestershire, GL5 4EP

www.amberley-books.com

British Library Cataloguing in Publication Data.
A catalogue record for this book is available from the British Library.

ISBN 978 1 4456 3309 1 (print)
978 1 4456 3326 8 (ebook)

Typeset in 10pt on 12pt Sabon.
Typesetting and Origination by Amberley Publishing.
Printed in the UK.

Contents

Introduction

Terry Jones, of *Monty Python* fame, came to live in Colwyn Bay with his mother and brother when he was a little boy during the Second World War, but by and large this town has not been the home of famous men and women. However, for better or worse, we all influence those with whom we live, and through the ages the people of Colwyn Bay have shown consideration and love, and sadly, centuries ago, some cruelty towards their fellow inhabitants. George Eliot's great fanfare for the silent majority resonates still, and could apply to this town:

> For the growing good of the world is partly dependent on unhistoric acts; and that things are not so ill with you and me as they might have been, is half owing to the number who lived faithfully a hidden life, and rest in unvisited tombs.

When we close our eyes and remember our home town, do we remember the streets and the buildings, or are our thoughts drawn to the people who lived there? Is a place important to us because of its atmosphere, or do we hanker after our old friends? I suspect the colour of our memories is made brilliant by the people who still stalk our subconscious minds. The history of Colwyn Bay is unique, as is the history of any town, because of the people who formed it and imprinted their personalities upon it, and who help us to be more aware of the chain of links over the generations.

The Romans marched through Colwyn Bay, Sir David Erskine lived in Erskine House (now Rydal Penrhos Junior School) and held sway over large tracts of this land and its people, architects influenced the style of the place, and Welsh princes lauded it over everyone. We, all of us, over the course of our lives, by the very nature of our personalities and actions, preach a sermon that others either follow or reject. But nevertheless, that sermon imprints itself on the way we view our town. Teenage soldiers dying in muddy Flanders fields shouted out not for the memory of their home villages, but for their mothers.

Four hundred years ago, John Donne wrote a poem called 'Good Friday, 1613, Riding Westward'. He imagines that he is riding to the west, away from Jesus, who will rise in the east and be subjected to suffering the poet does not wish to witness. There is a couplet in the poem that still resonates today: 'Though these things, as I ride, be from mine eye,/They are present yet unto my memory.' He was writing at a time when many important matters were present in the memory of almost every human being. Today we do not live in such a culture, and so we have to be reminded of our forebears. The old should cultivate the friendship of the young, for in so doing they help to perpetuate the connection with our history.

Tracing human recollection is fascinating, and this book is a patchwork woven together by princes, clergymen, teachers, writers, sportsmen, landowners, soldiers, photographers, inventors, architects, entertainers, kings, and many more, all of whom add variety and enjoyment to our memories of Colwyn Bay.

Daniel Allen, 1838–1904

Mr Allen was the founder of the prestigious department store, Daniel Allen & Sons, on Station Road, thus his association with Colwyn Bay dated back to the early history of the town. He originally opened his business in Leek, Staffordshire, but arrived in Colwyn Bay in 1879 and opened the store on Station Road, living with his wife, Margaret, in a flat above the business. Between 1862 and 1878, the couple had seven children – four boys and three girls – all of whom eventually became partners in the thriving business. His obituary notice alludes to the fact, which today would seem incongruous to highlight, that he 'had the distinction of being one of the first conservatives to come to reside in Colwyn Bay'. He was the churchwarden of the temporary church of St Paul's at the time when the original building had been destroyed by fire, and while the present John Douglas-designed edifice was being built. He was, it was reported, 'of a singularly quiet and retiring disposition, but was never the less respected for his straightforward and sterling character'. The store remained one of the premiere shopping attractions in Wales (along with W. S. Wood's further up the road) up until 1971 when, eight years short of its century, the store was closed forever. The world and society had changed; people's methods of shopping had altered over the years and two World Wars had changed everything. The goods on offer in the store were no longer attractive to a more fractured society. The large, distinctive building that Mr Allen erected still stands on Station Road and now houses The Original Factory Shop.

Daniel Allen and family, from left: Edward, Edgar, Elizabeth, Daniel, Clara, Elizabeth, Alfred, Daniel (jnr), Gertrude.

How Herr Aucher's houses looked originally.

How Herr Aucher's houses look today.

Herr R. W. Fitz Aucher, *c.* 1908 – *c.* 1973

Fitz Aucher was a German who somehow had become friendly with the Lord Hesketh, who had developed much of Abergele and owned Gwrych Castle. In 1938, Herr Aucher formed the Aucher Estates Limited and the Llysfaen Development Company Limited; the former to hold the land, the latter to develop it. It was an imaginative and enlightened attempt to build affordable, semi-detached housing in Llysfaen. Unusually for those days, there was to be running hot and cold water with indoor toilets and gardens. There was to be a free insurance scheme and social amenities available on the estate. Each house was to have a coal bunker and a larder, there was a variety of coloured roof tiles on offer, and you could have your house painted any colour you desired. Herr Aucher employed Arthur Clayton of Manchester as his architect. In the estate brochure he wrote: 'We in Llysfaen are fortunate in possessing natural beauty and our appreciation of this beauty is too sincere to allow the intrusion of any so called enterprise that might spoil the countryside.' Herr Aucher captured the mood of the pre-war times, and used his skills to develop his business. The houses he built are still there today along Gadlas Road, Cynfran Road and the cul-de-sac of Gamar Road. Just before the Second World War, it was a bold flight of imagination for a German national to develop a private housing estate in a place like Llysfaen. But for Herr Aucher the timing was fatal. Because of his nationality, he was detained and interned on the Isle of Man for the duration of the war, and after that he seems to have faded anonymously into the mists of time.

Sergeant Arthur Banks GC, RAF, VR, 6 October 1923 – 20 December 1944

Arthur Banks was born in Llanddulas. Twenty-one years later, he was tortured by the Germans and murdered by the Italian Fascists. He is buried in Argenta Gap War Cemetery in Italy, a long way from the town of his birth. There is, however, a commemorative stone in his memory on the war memorial at Llanddulas. King George VI presented Arthur's George Medal to Arthur's father, Capt. Charles Banks, who had been awarded the Distinguished Flying Cross for his service during the First World War, at Buckingham Place in December 1948. Sgt Banks had been shot down over Northern Italy while undertaking an armed reconnaissance operation in a Mustang. He tried to get back to the Allied lines and made contact with a partisan group. In December 1944, while attempting to resupply the partisans, he was betrayed and captured by the Germans. Over the next few days he was tortured by both the Germans and the Italians, but he remained silent. He was then stripped, doused in petrol, set alight and weighted down, before being thrown into the River Po. He managed to survive and swam to the riverbank, where he was recaptured by the Brigate Nere (Italian Fascists) and then shot in the head by Lt Turati. On such unimaginable bravery does our freedom rest.

IN MEMORY OF THOSE FROM
THE PARISH OF LLANDDULAS
WHO FELL IN THE WAR 1914-19.

L.CPL. GWILYM JONES	R.W.F.
L.CPL. SGT. JOHN JONES	R.W.F.
JOHN DAVIES	R.W.F.
ROBERT DAVIES	R.W.F.
2ND LIEUT. ARTHUR C. BARES	R.W.F.
LIEUT. CHARLES J. CADMAN, M.C.	R.E.
DAVID LEWIS WILLIAMS	M.T.
WILLIAM ROBERTS	R.W.E.
WILLIAM ROBERTS	R.N.

Y MAE EU HENW YN BYW BYTH.
THEIR NAME LIVETH FOR EVERMORE.

1939 —— 1945

SGT.PILOT RICHARD J. DAVIES	R.A.F.V.R.
CPL.IVOR J. GRIFFITHS	R.SIGNALS.
1/SGT PERCIVAL H.M. JONES, D.F.M.	R.A.F.
A.B. IEUAN LLOYD	R.N.
A.C.1 ROBERT MORRIS	R.A.F.
GUNNER ROBERT B. ROGERS	WELSH GDS.
CPL. DYFRIG WILLIAMS	R.E.
GNR. GRIFFITH WILLIAMS	R.A.

Left and below:
Llanddulas War Memorial.

Sydney Francis Barnes, 19 April 1873 – 26 December 1967

Sydney Barnes was born in a house on Penrhyn Avenue, Rhos-on-Sea, and is generally regarded as one of the best bowlers in the history of cricket. He took 1,432 wickets for Staffordshire at less than nine runs each, and played for the county until he was sixty-one. He played for England on twenty-seven occasions. In 1911, he enabled England to win the Ashes when he took thirty-four wickets in the series against Australia. In 1963, in the 100th edition of *Wisden Cricketers' Almanack*, Sydney Barnes was named as one of its 'Six Giants of the Wisden Century'. He is the only player to have ever played for both England and Wales; between 1923 and 1930, Wales had an official team for which he played in nine matches. He qualified to play for Wales because at the time he was living in Colwyn Bay, and when the Colwyn Bay Cricket Club ground on Penrhyn Avenue was opened in 1924, he acted as a coach in the nets. In 1929, he played against South Africa at Rydal School while he managed The Royal public house on Abergele Road. For some reason, now fortunately lost in the mist of time, on one occasion his pub licence was withheld. This may indicate an aspect of Barnes' character that Archie MacLaren discovered when, as captain, he chose Sydney Barnes to join the England team to tour Australia; when the ship on which the team was travelling seemed in danger of sinking, Archie Maclaren declared, 'Well, there's one comfort, if we do go down that bastard Barnes goes down with us.'

The Royal Hotel, *c.* 1910.

Alfred Bestall MBE, 1892–1986

Alfred Bestall was the son of Methodist missionaries who were serving in Mandalay, Burma, at the time of his birth. Twelve years later, probably because of its Methodist foundation, he was living in Colwyn Bay at Rydal Mount School. He spent the next seven years in Colwyn Bay, where he excelled academically in mathematics and the classics. However, he was always getting into trouble for doodling in his exercise books, and he became involved in the artwork of the school theatrical productions. The doodling and artwork were the first intimations of his future creative work on the Rupert Bear strip in the *Daily Express*. While in his last year at Rydal Mount School, his parents took him for holidays to Trefriw, in the Conwy Valley. It was from these jaunts that he developed his love of the Snowdonia hills, and many of the backgrounds to his Rupert Bear stories are based on the landscape of Snowdonia. During the First World War, he served as a soldier in Flanders and transported troops around the battlefields in a red, double-decker London bus. Each year, after the war, he stayed at Penrhiwgoch (Snowdon Views) in Nant Gwynant. In 1935, he took over the stories and artwork of the Rupert Bear strip from May Tourtel, and he improved the stories by centring them around normal daily life and making Rupert more human. He continued with this work for the next thirty years, during which time the Rupert Bear Annual became an enjoyable and important part of many children's Christmases. Mr Bestall always coloured the cover painting of the annuals, but his black and white drawings inside the annuals were coloured by 'Rupert Artists'. While he is remembered lovingly as the author and illustrator of Rupert Bear, he was more proud of his work for Punch, his double watercolour pictures in Tatler, and for two oil paintings, which were hung in the Royal Academy. In 1958, he bought a cottage in Beddgelert, which he named Penlan, and in 1980 it became his permanent home. It was here that he was visited by Paul McCartney and his family after McCartney had composed 'The Frog Song', based on Mr Bestall's drawing 'The Frogs' Chorus'. Seventy years after moving to Colwyn Bay, Mr Bestall died on 15 January 1986, aged ninety-three, at a nursing home in Porthmadog.

Dr Constance Mary Bevan MB, ChB, DCP, DTM, 1925–2004

In Mochdre there are roads named Bevan Avenue, Oxwich Road and Gower Road, all christened by the Bevan family. In 1937, there were just two large semi-detached houses on Bevan Avenue, Overton (now No. 7) and Mewslade (now No. 2, Gower Road). George Bevan lived in Overton, while his son George Jnr, daughter-in-law Constance Alice and granddaughter Constance Mary, lived next door in Mewslade. Mr Bevan and his son ran an ironmongery, plumbing and electrical business at No. 36 Princes Drive in Colwyn Bay. The family had arrived here from the Gower Peninsular in South Wales, where there are two spectacularly beautiful bays, Overton and Mewslade, and where you find Oxwich Castle. Mary was a clever, outdoor sort of girl, who loved the countryside and enjoyed playing golf. In 1950, she qualified as a doctor,

Dr Constance Bevan, 1950.

which was unusual for those days, and eventually became a consultant pathologist. After her mother died, she left Britain and sailed, via America, to Australia, where she remained for the rest of her life, working for some years in Melbourne and eventually becoming an eminent member of the Mildura Base Hospital medical team. Dr Bevan died in April 2004, and in her will her last stated wish was that her ashes should be scattered on the Gower Peninsula, a wish that was carried out by an old childhood friend, Barbara Armitage, the daughter of William Wood, the owner of Wood's Department Store on Station Road.

Donald Boumphrey MC, 4 October 1892 – 12 September 1971

Donald Boumphrey, born in Birkenhead, was a schoolmaster at Rydal School, teaching Latin and mathematics, from 1924 to 1962. Before the First World War, he was himself a schoolboy at Shrewsbury School, and went on to win the Military Cross in the awful, bloody battles of the Somme and Passchendaele. He had been an outstanding rugby and cricket player, playing minor county cricket for Cheshire and Denbighshire, and had it not been for the war he would, in all probability, have played for his country; he did play once for Wales against the West Indies and was bowled out in his second innings by Learie Constantine. Neville Cardus described him as 'the best amateur batsman

Rydal School, 1958. Donald Boumphrey is the bald-headed man in the front row, to the left of Ken Cooper, who is in the sweater. The author is in the second row from the back, fourth from the right.

in England'. By 1924 he was the housemaster of Glanaber House, a Rydal School boarding house, and he was in charge of rugby and cricket at the school. In 1926, a fourteen-year-old boy called Wilfred Wooller joined Glanabber House, and in later life recalled, 'Boumphrey's paternal manner made me feel immediately at home and I can still remember Boumphrey would often wander into our dormitory before lights out and talk at length about sport.' It was due to Mr Boumphreys's initial enthusiasm for sport, and eagerness for the thrill, excitement and exhilaration that sport engenders in some children, that Wilfred Wooller became an international rugby and cricket player. The same happened to Bleddyn Williams a few years later when he also came under the benevolent eye of Mr Boumphrey. His retirement in 1962 was marked by a moving ceremony in the Rydal School Memorial Hall, at which this writer was present, when, to a standing ovation, he walked slowly and with great dignity down the aisle of the hall and out into a half-forgotten retirement in a room put aside for him in the school. It is on the broad shoulders and unselfish natures of such forgotten, modest men, that the future reputations and worldly success of others is based.

Eric Bramall, 1927–1996

Eric Bramall was once described by journalist Roger Wilkes as 'a life force'. He brought enormous enjoyment and delight to many thousands of people through his love and expertise with puppetry. He was born in Wallasey, and was fascinated with marionettes from an early age. In due course, he created his own puppet shows, which became a regular feature of seaside variety shows. After the Second World War, he performed his show for two seasons in the Colwyn Bay Pier Pavilion, and in the 1950s his productions became a regular feature of the entertainment in Eirias Park.

Eric Bramall, *c.* 1970.

The Puppet Theatre today.

With the help of the town clerk, Geoffrey Edwards, he moved into a purpose-built wooden structure opposite Rhos Point. In 1958, with the generous support of the Ford family of Aberhod, he transformed one of the outbuildings on the Rhos-on-Sea promenade at Aberhod into the first permanent Harlequin Puppet Theatre in Great Britain. The architect of the theatre was Gwilym Parry Davies, and his design won a Civic Trust Award. The theatre was directed by Mr Bramall from its creation until his death, a span of thirty-eight years, a time through which he made the puppets and scenery for over forty productions. Chris Somerville, a close associate of Eric Bramall for many years, is now the sole director of the theatre. Mr Bramall pioneered the spectacle of floorshow puppetry or marionette cabaret, a style of presentation that demands superb manipulation, where a marionette is manipulated without stage or scenery in full view of the audience. He, along with Somerville, was responsible for Britain's first ever International Puppet Festival, held in Colwyn Bay in 1963 and 1968. He edited the Marionette Guild's first yearbook in 1955, and wrote two books – *Making a Start with Marionettes* and *Puppet Plays and Playwriting* – and was an honorary member of the Royal Cambrian Academy. Chris Somerville described his friend as 'a happy man who lived a happy life with great enthusiasm'. He also contributed enormously, through his mastery of puppetry technique, to the popularity of Colwyn Bay and Rhos-on-Sea.

Scholto Elizabeth Brandenburgh, 1912–2000

Scholto Brandenburgh was a German lady who in 1939, at the insistence of Constance Smith, the headmistress of Penrhos College for girls, was able to get out of Germany on one of the last passenger aeroplanes to leave the country before the start of hostilities. Her parents were wealthy aristocrats and had sent Scholto and her sister to the school before the war, but Scholto decided that she wanted to teach there as well. The headmistress cabled her to travel to Derbyshire and not Colwyn Bay, because the school had taken up residence in the home of the Duke of Devonshire, Chatsworth House, while its own home was taken over by the Ministry of Food. Miss Brandenbugh was billeted in a house in the local village, the owners of which accused her of signalling to German bombers by leaving the curtains open and the light on at night. When the first group of Jewish girls arrived as refugees from Germany, one young girl announced that she was not willing to go into Miss Brandenbugh's schoolhouse because she was German. Miss Brandenbugh, who was a very tall lady and who had overheard the remark, went up to the girl, put her hand on her shoulder and said, 'Yes you are young lady', and that was that. Many years later this same girl, then a married woman, returned to the school to apologise to Miss Brandenburgh for her hurtful teenage remark. Miss Brandenburgh remained at the school for the rest of her teaching career, returning to Colwyn Bay when the Ministry of Food packed up and returned to London after the war. She retired in 1980 and went to live with another Penrhos teacher, Miss Ankers, at Stoneleigh, St George's Road, in Rhos-on-Sea. Miss Brandenburgh was born on the 5 November, Bon Fire Night, which was wholly appropriate as she was a firecracker of a lady.

Scholto Brandenburgh, *c.* 1916, with her parents and grandfather. Her father was killed by an Allied bomb.

Rhos-on-Sea swimming pool, *c.* 1965.

The swimming pool was Mr Breese's domain.

Matthew Breese, 1903–1996

Matthew Breese was the manager of the Rhos-on-Sea swimming pool from before it was officially opened in 1933 by British boxing champion Jack Peterson, to the day the council bought it in 1965. He was born in Old Colwyn, but moved to Rhyl with his parents, who ran a dairy; they had one cow in the back garden that was changed every few weeks. It was in Rhyl that he met his future wife, Florence, in St Thomas' church where his father was the choirmaster. He was a keen sportsman, good at boxing, tennis and swimming, being the captain of his swimming team and gaining the sidestroke British record for a short while. He was also a keen musician, playing the clarinet in a local band. He was good at nurturing young swimmers, and when he managed the pool at Rhos-on-Sea he trained Enid Sofe, the future triple Welsh diving champion. The swimming pool was a private business. Mr Towne, the owner of the Tan-y-Bryn Hotel, was the chairman of the Trustees, and it was he who invited Mr Breese to become the manager of the newly opened facility. The water in the pool was pumped in from the sea, under the promenade and the Rhos Abbey Hotel, purified and pumped back out to the sea. During the Second World War, Mr Breese was an RAF physical training instructor and ended up in Germany at the end of the conflict. While he was away, his wife Florence looked after the running of the pool. After the end of the war until the late 1960s, children by and large did as they were told. Mr Breese was a large, fit man who the youngsters respected, and many parents would say 'we know our children are safe with Mr Breese'. From 1.00 p.m. to 2.15 p.m., everyone had to get out of the water while he had his lunch, as he was also the lifeguard, and everyone obeyed the rule. He always wore plastic sandals, which he bought from Lillywhites of London, because the chlorine did not rot them. The pool closed at 9.00 p.m., which he announced by ringing a large school-like handbell. His son, Mike, bought an African Grey Parrot for him from Africa, an excellent mimic, which he would take out onto the poolside in the evenings. The parrot, called Coko, would mimic the bell and squawk 'all out' in Mr Breese's voice. In the evenings, at the height of summer, he organised comedy galas, when a member of the audience was invited to swim across the pool against a professional swimmer. Unbeknownst to the amateur swimmer, the professional would be holding on to an underwater stirrup attached to a rope, which was pulled across the pool by a gaggle of lads and made the professional swimmer look something like a racing submarine. In 1965, he went to manage the newly opened Rydal School swimming pool, and eventually retired to live in Mauldeth Road in Rhos-on-Sea. In due course, he and Florence went to live with their son Mike and his family in Bridgnorth, which is where he peacefully ended his days.

Revd Isaiah Brookes-Jones, 1884–1907

When the Revd Brookes-Jones' father died in 1887, his mother brought him and her five other children to Colwyn Bay, where she let rooms to policemen and summer visitors. On 21 September 1905, when he was twenty-one years old, Isaiah set sail,

Revd Isaiah Brookes-Jones.

with his mother's blessing, for Canada, where he started to minister to the Cree Indians in Manitoba. He learnt the Cree language and travelled by canoe up and down Lake Winnipeg. Two months after arriving in Canada, he was with the Sioux Indians at Oak Lake Indian Reserve, north of the Assiniboine River, and wrote home that, 'They looked beautiful in their coloured blankets … These are the refugees from the Minnesota Massacre about 40 years ago.' By 1907, he was translating Welsh hymns into Cree for the wedding of William Bradburn and Anabella Le Claire. On 28 November 1907, while learning to swim in the YMCA pool in Winnipeg, he drowned. The principal of Wesley College instructed that his body be buried among the 'civilised people' of Winnipeg, and so it was that he was interred in Elmwood Cemetery, thousands of miles away from his home in Colwyn Bay. A picture of him still hangs in the church room of Horeb Welsh Methodist chapel on Rhiw Road, Colwyn Bay, where as a young man he, his mother and his siblings all attended the services.

Will Catlin, 1871–1953

Will Catlin, originally called William Fox, was born in Leicester. He was the first man to bring entertainment to the people of Colwyn Bay. His original troupe of players used to perform in tents on beaches or on promenades at numerous seaside resorts. It could be a hard life for the players; the open-air performances tempted their audiences to stay for the show, but depart before anyone could come around with the collecting box. This is why Mr Catlin began to book his pierrots into covered theatres – in Whitley Bay in 1908 as 'Catlin's Royal Pierrots', and in the Arcadia Theatre in Scarborough where he was booked to amuse the town people during the First World War. He was a firm 'governor', a stickler as an employer, and would make sure that his pierrots whitened their shoes every day and that their costumes were kept in pristine condition. In 1915, he bought the theatre that stood on the present site of Venue Cymru in Llandudno, and which he renamed the Arcadia. He was an impressive character, with his ever-present cigar clenched firmly between his fingers. In the late 1920s, he bought a small plot of land on the grass embankment below the Colwyn Bay railway station, which runs down to the promenade between the pier and Marine Drive. He carved out a lay-by into the embankment, and built an open-air stage with a small roof. His pierrots had to change in their digs and then walk down to the 'theatre', the clever idea being that this walk would advertise the show. It was Will Catlin who commissioned and built the Arcadia Theatre on Princes Drive in Colwyn Bay. Sidney Colwyn Foulkes, a new and very young architect in Colwyn Bay, wrote to Mr Catlin emphasising his professional qualifications for the Arcadia project. When Mr Catlin stepped off the train at Colwyn Bay station to meet his new architect, he was amazed to find such a young person. Nevertheless the two of them got on well together, and the project was completed. The theatre remained in place until the construction of the A55 through the town, and it had to be destroyed in February 1981.

Catlin's Pierrots, Colwyn Bay, 1911.

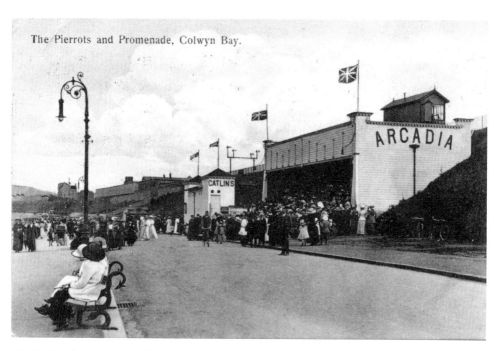

Mr Catlin's first theatre in Colwyn Bay.

Sir George Cayley, 6th Baronet, 27 December 1773 – 15 December 1857

The Cayley Promenade and the Cayley pub in Rhos-on-Sea are named after the Cayley family, and specifically after Sir George Cayley. The pub sign hanging from the Cayley is an acknowledgement of Sir George's importance in the history of aeronautics, as well as being a delightfully produced piece of 'pub art'. He was the man who identified the four vector forces that influenced an aircraft: thrust, lift, drag and gravity. Sometime before 1849 he designed and built a biplane, the first to carry a human aloft, and persuaded his coachman to fly it on his Brompton estate (hence Brompton Avenue, Rhos-on-Sea) in Yorkshire. His London home, identified by a blue plaque on the wall, was at No. 20 Hertford Street in Shepherd's Market, just behind the Hilton Hotel. His pioneering work was acknowledged by the Wright brothers. He stressed the importance of lightness when building his machines, and realised that for the landing gear it was tension, not compression that was necessary, and so used string as wires for this job. This wire wheel idea is still used today for bicycles, cars and many other vehicles. He also invented self-righting lifeboats, caterpillar tractors and seat belts. As well as owning a lot of land in Rhos-on-Sea, the family also owned land at Llannerch, St Asaph, thus we have Llannerch Roads East and West in Rhos today. Sir Georges's son was called Sir Digby Cayley, and gave his name to Digby Road. The 8th Baronet was christened Sir George Allanson Cayley, and left behind Allanson Road as a memorial. He called his son (the 9th Baronet) Sir George Everard Arthur Cayley, after whom Everard Road is named. The 10th Baronet was called Sir Kenelm Henry Ernest Cayley, and we have Kenelm Road today in Rhos-on-Sea.

Cayley Arms pub sign today.

Mr Clough's home that became a school.

Old Colwyn in Mr Clough's time.

Richard Butler Clough, *c.* 1790–1844

Richard Butler Clough was the grandson of Hugh Clough of Plas Clough, Denbigh. He was a man of wealth and status who had bought an old farmhouse, known originally as Colwyn Farm, near the present Min-y-Don Park, Old Colwyn, and transformed it into Min-y-Don Hall. There was a bell hanging over the coach yard, which summoned the servants to their meals and informed the inhabitants of the small village of Colwyn (now Old Colwyn) of the time of day. He was descended from Sir Richard Clough, who served Queen Elizabeth I, and worked with Sir Thomas Gresham in the founding of the London Royal Exchange. Richard Butler Clough was a wealthy merchant from Liverpool who imported coal into Old Colwyn via Beach Road (then known as Glan-y-Mor Road), and charged a 6*d* toll to any vehicle using that route. He also built a mill on the road to grind the gorse from the bushes growing nearby, to feed his horses. He married his cousin Catherine, and while he was the churchwarden at Llandrillo-yn-Rhos church, the communion plate was stolen; the thief was caught in Liverpool and received a sentence of seven years transportation. Mr Clough helped to build St Catherine's church, Old Colwyn (named after St Catherine of Alexandria, because she had the same name as his wife), and when he died a window was placed at the eastern end of the church in his memory. Now, 176 years later, the church is closed. Min-y-Don Hall was demolished in 1939, and all that remains is the original coach house, which has been converted into a modern house, Cwrt Bach, on the bend of Min-y-Don Road.

Alvin Langdon Coburn, 11 June 1882 – 23 November 1966

For the last twenty years of his life, Alvin Langdon Coburn lived at Awen, Ebberston Road East, in Rhos-on-Sea. He named the house Awen because 'Awen' is a Welsh word used to denote poetic inspiration, and is historically used to describe the divine inspiration attributed to Welsh bards, of which he was one. He is buried in Llandrillo-yn-Rhos parish churchyard, alongside his wife, Edith, who died on their forty-fifth wedding anniversary. Alvin Langdon Coburn was an American world-renowned photographer who was a key figure in the development of American pictorialism. He was born in Boston, and in 1890 he and his mother (his father died when Alvin was seven years old) visited his mother's brothers, who gave him a 4x5 Kodak camera, which sparked his lifetime's interest and work. In 1899, when he was seventeen, he visited London and nine of his prints were accepted for the Royal Photographic Society. In 1900, when he became a member of an association of artistic photographers, the Linked Ring, he was elevated to the ranks of the most elite photographers of the day. In 1904, he was commissioned by *The Metropolitan Magazine* to photograph England's leading artists and writers, including G. K. Chesterton, H. G. Wells and George Bernard Shaw, who described Coburn as 'one of the most sensitive artist photographers now living'. He became a British subject in 1932, after having lived in the country for over twenty years. In the 1930s, he was much influenced by a quasi-religious sect known as the Universal Order, which someone described as being 'devoted to synthetic

Alvin Langdon Coburn.

philosophy'. He became a Mason, joined the Trillo Lodge in Colwyn Bay, and set up his own small lodge room in a bedroom at Awen.

Air Marshal Henry George Crowe CBE, MC, JP, 1897–1983

In 1910, when Irish-born Henry George Crowe was thirteen years old, he went to school at Myndon Hall School on Station Road, Old Colwyn. We now refer to the area as Min-y-Don. The building, originally christened Bod Difyr and built in 1899, still stands on the corner of Cefn Road and Station Road. The headmaster was Henry Elias Mocatta, who would have been a businessman and saw the opportunity to make money by educating the children of the richer classes. There were many such schools dotted around the Colwyn Bay area. Four years after arriving in Colwyn Bay, George landed at the Royal Military College, Sandhurst. During the First World War, he became a flying ace and was credited with eight aerial victories. In April 1918, he was shot down by anti-aircraft fire, which totally destroyed his Bristol F.2 Fighter. Ten days later, he returned from a special mission with his plane riddled with bullet holes. He was shot down six times in eleven days, but remained unscathed. When the Second World War began, he was deputy director of War Training and Tactics, and was then sent to India where he was made an acting Air Vice-Marshal, and was instrumental in organising the air cover for General Slim and the 'Forgotten Army' fighting the Japanese in the jungles of Burma. In 1944, he took command of No. 223 Group at Peshawar. When he received his Military Cross in 1918, it was written in the *London Gazette* that he received the honour 'for conspicuous gallantry and devotion to duty when taking part in many low-flying bomb raids ... On three occasions his machine was shot down by enemy fire, but he continued his work, and his great fearlessness and fine spirit have been an invaluable example to others.' Not bad for a lad taught in Old Colwyn.

Minydon Hall, 1905.

Minydon Hall today.

Air Marshal Sir Denis Crowley-Milling, KCB, CBE, DSO, DFC and Bar, 1919–1996

Sir Denis was brought up in Colwyn Bay, first at Westbury on the promenade and then at a house called Belmont on Pen-y-Bryn Road. He was educated locally before moving on to Malvern College. In later years, his mother had the roof of Belmont painted red so that he could identify it when he flew over it. Both his parents are buried in Llandrillo-yn-Rhos parish churchyard. Right up until her death, Sir Denis always kept in touch with his childhood nanny, Mrs Guard, who lived in a tiny house on Church Road, Rhos-on-Sea; a thoughtfulness that meant a lot to her. During the Second World War, he was a fighter pilot flying from RAF Coltishall as number two to his commanding officer, Douglas Bader. While at Coltishall, he was credited with destroying eight enemy aircraft. In August 1941, he was shot down over France while escorting Stirling bombers on a raid over Lille. With the help of the French Resistance, he evaded capture, made his way back to Britain and rejoined his squadron. After the war, in 1947, he became a squadron leader, and from 1962 to 1964 he was in command of RAF Leconfield. In retirement, he was the master of the Guild of Air Pilots and registrar and secretary of the Order of the Bath.

Air Marshal Sir Denis Crowley-Milling.

Cuneglas, Cynlas Goch, Early Sixth Century

Cynlas Goch (Cynlas the Red) was the son of Owain Danwyn, who is a popular contender as the historical King Arthur. Cynlas was a King of Rhos, who built his fortress on the summit of Bryn Euryn, the rubble and foundations of which can still be made out today. The fortress was well constructed, with at least a 3-metre high wall and a 3½-metre thick rampart. The layout matches the similar fortress at Garn Boduan on the Llyn Peninsular, and the fort at Pen-y-Castell on a rocky ridge high above Maenan. Cynlas was not like his father; in fact he was a terror who abandoned his wife to marry her sister, whom he dragged from a nunnery. The monk Gildas the Wise, writing at the time, described him thus: 'You contempter of God and vilifier of his order.' Others referred to him as the 'Red Butcher', and his domain is still called Dinerth from the medieval Welsh 'Din Eirth', meaning Bear's Fort. Cynlas' kingdom stretched from the Great Orme to the Creuddyn Peninsular, down the Vale of Clwyd and south along the east bank of the River Conwy, over which he held sway from the top of Bryn Euryn, where he was ensconced in what was known as his 'Bear's Den'.

Bryn Euryn, Cynlas Goch's fortress.

William Davis' memorial at Beaumaris.

Blessed William Davis, 1556–1593

William Davis was the first priest martyred for his faith in Wales. He was born at Croes-yn-Eirias, which we now know as the area boarded by the main entrance to Eirias Park on one side and Groes Road on the other, with Abergele Road running through it. In the mid-sixteenth century, this was a small, isolated rural community. He was a bright boy and went on to St Edmund's Hall, Oxford, and then on to the seminary at Rheims, France, where he was ordained as a Catholic priest in 1585, aged twenty nine. Queen Elizabeth I was on the throne of England and introduced harsh penal laws against Catholics, and most priests had been banished, imprisoned, tortured and put to death. Spies, many of whom were well established along the London to Holyhead route that led to Ireland, helped her find these Catholic priests. Undeterred, Father William Davis returned to Colwyn Bay in 1585 and ministered to the North Wales community, where he was helped by his Catholic friend Robert Pugh of Plas Penrhyn, which is now known as Penrhyn Old Hall, Penrhyn Bay. For a time, he took refuge in a cave on the cliffs of the Little Orme, where he produced a devotional book, *The Christian Mirror*. Eventually, while in Holyhead arranging for students to sail to Spain, he was arrested and taken to Beaumaris. He refused to take the Oath of Supremacy acknowledging the Queen as head of the Church, and so was found guilty. The judges were fearful of the Catholic sympathies of the Beaumaris people and so took him to prisons in Shropshire and Worcester, before finally returning him to Anglesey. Hangmen had to come from Chester, and they were stoned on their arrival and refused shelter or food. The gallows were built in the grounds of Beaumaris Castle so that the townspeople could be kept well away from the scene of the execution. He died bravely, kissing and blessing the noose before it was put around his neck, and telling the small crowd of officials that his 'blood would bleed for the Isle of Anglesey'. He was aged thirty-seven. There is now a shrine and plaque in memory of Blessed William Davis in the church of Our Lady of Martyrs next door to Beaumaris Castle.

Oscar Deutsch, 1893–1941

Oscar Deutsch was born in Balsall, Birmingham. His father was a Jewish scrap merchant and his mother was a Polish immigrant. He was the inspiration and moving force behind the Odeon cinema chain. He liked to tell everyone that the name Odeon was the result of allowing each letter to start the words, 'Oscar Deutsch Entertains Our Nation'. He was a generous and sentimental man, and offered his staff interest-free loans when they got into debt. In the ten years up to his death during the Second World War, he built 258 Odeon cinemas. One of his best was on the corner of Conwy Road and Marine Road on the opposite corner from St John's Methodist church, where today you will find the Swn-y-Mor flats. It replaced Erskine Lodge, one of the two original ornate gatehouses built at the end of St David Erskine's driveway, which is now Pwllycrochan Avenue. Mr Deutsch's architect, Cecil Clavering, an employee of

Harry Weedon (1887–1970), was a racy character and a talented pianist, who had served in the Royal Flying Corps during the First World War. It was he who in 1936 created the glamorous, eye-catching Art Deco decoration in the Colwyn Bay Odeon auditorium. Mrs Deutsch felt that this particular decoration was her favourite of all her husband's cinemas, and yet the Colwyn Bay Odeon was one of the cheapest he ever built. During the war, servicemen home from the front line of battle, teachers, nurses and the typists and clerks from the Ministry of Food based in Colwyn Bay, for 1/- (5p) could wallow in their futuristic dreams in a futuristic building thanks to Oscar Deutsch. Oscar Deutsch's cousin was Arnold Deutsch, who was the Russian controller of the five spies, Philby, Burgess, Maclean, Blunt and Cairncross.

This and next page: Odeon Cinema, Colwyn Bay.

John Douglas, 1830–1911

John Douglas was an architect with his own practice at No. 6 Abbey Square in Chester. His maternal grandfather was the village blacksmith in Eccleston, and his father was a builder and joiner. In 1860, he married Elizabeth Edmunds, a farmer's daughter, in a church that in later life he was to restore. They had five children, but sadly only two of them survived into adulthood. The architectural historian Edward Hubbard wrote that Mr Douglas' life 'seems to have been one of thorough devotion to architecture … which may well have intensified by the death of this wife and other domestic worries'. His work is of particular interest because of the importance he felt joinery and highly detailed woodcarving should play in his church designs, and the impact it had on the landscape of Colwyn Bay. He designed St Paul's church on the corner of Rhiw Road and Abergele Road, Christ Church (known locally as the Cathedral of the Hills) in Bryn-y-Maen, St John the Baptist church on Station Road, Old Colwyn, St David's Welsh church on Rhiw Road (next door to St Paul's church), and both St Paul's vicarage and Christ Church vicarage, Llety Drew (on Abergele Road beside the approach to the Colwyn Bay Civic Centre). Only one of his buildings has been demolished; the Colwyn Bay Hotel in 1974/75 (now the site of Princess Court on the corner of Marine Road and The Promenade). When Mr D. R. Thomas visited Colwyn Bay 1857, the only building he saw was one cottage and a toll bar. However eight years later, with the sale of Lady Erskine's Pwllycrochan Estate, the area began to be developed as a resort. Sir John Pender, a Glasgow merchant, bought the estate and his preferred architect was John Douglas. The pair of them made a triumphant visit to the town in 1872, and the train was greeted with flags, cheering crowds and a military band. By this time, Mr Douglas' vision for the new hotel on the promenade was nearing completion. Douglas lived to see the completion of all his churches, vicarages and houses in Colwyn Bay, and our town is the better for his inspiration and hard work.

Colywn Bay Hotel, designed by John Douglas, *c.* 1890.

David Geoffrey Edwards MBE, LLB, 1920–2004

John Roberts, the clerk to the Bay of Colwyn Town Council at the time of Geoffrey Edwards' death, described him as 'Mr Colwyn Bay', while in the *North Wales Weekly News* it was written that he was 'one of the town's most influential pioneers'. He was a solicitor and town clerk to the Colwyn Bay Borough Council from 1962 to 1974, and the chief executive of the Conwy County Borough Council from 1974 to 1981. He was vice president of the Llangollen International Musical Eisteddfod, an honorary fellow of Conwy's Royal Cambrian Academy, and chairman of the Welsh Mountain Zoo Trustees, having been influential behind the scenes in persuading Mr Jackson to open his zoo at the Flagstaff Gardens in Colwyn Bay. He was vice chairman of both Eirias High School and Llandrillo College. He was the driving force behind the acquisition of Glan-y-Don and its parkland in Old Colwyn, and engineered the move, in 1964, of the council offices from the old site on the corner of Coed Pella and Abergele Roads in the middle of the town, to this new, more fitting and commodious site, known as The Civic Centre. Mr Edwards, almost single-handedly, negotiated the sale of some of the Glan-y-Don land for £18,000 to the North Wales police for their new headquarters, and sold the old site in town for shops and offices, by which time Colwyn Bay had a new Civic Centre, which had cost just over £1,000. In 1984, he wrote the very readable *The Borough of Colwyn Bay*, which he billed as a social history of the Borough from 1934 to 1974. Mr Edwards' first wife, Kathleen, died in 1968 aged forty-eight. She had been born in Somerset, and he arranged for a box of earth from that county to be sent to him at the Civic Centre so that it could be spread around her casket when it was buried at Llandrillo-yn-Rhos parish churchyard. On the headstone of the grave he had inscribed: 'A lady of the West Country.' Later on, he married Noreen Thomas OBE, JP, the matron of Colwyn Bay Hospital, who was an influential person in her own right.

Outside Colwyn Bay Hotel, *c.* 1965. Geoffrey Edwards is in the front row, second from the left.

Sir David Erskine, 1st Baronet of Cambo, 1792–1841

David Erskine was born in Sweden and was a grandson of the 9th Earl of Kellie. In the early nineteenth century, while on the Continent he met Jane Silence Williams, who was on holiday there. They were married in 1821, when Jane was nineteen years old. By this time, Miss Silence had inherited Plas Isaf in Conway, and the Pwllycrochan Estate in Colwyn Bay from her father, the Revd Hugh Williams, who had died in 1809 at Pwllycrochan. Sir David and Lady Erskine decided to live at Pwllycrochan. The present Pwllycrochan building, which is now home to Rydal Penrhos Junior School, was, in Sir David Erskine's time, known as Erskine House, and was much smaller than the present building. Sir David had the original red-brick building pulled down and built an entirely new manor house, which is still the nucleus of the existing building. The house was the centre of a huge estate that covered most of what we now know as Colwyn Bay. Indeed, the present Pwllycrochan Avenue was originally Sir David's front drive. In the year of his marriage, on 27 August, Sir David was created the 1st Baronet of Cambo, and two years after his marriage he was elected High Sheriff for Denbighshire. He was a churchwarden, and his signature is in the minute book of the Llandrillo Vestry for a meeting held in August 1827. Sir David Erskine's wife had also inherited the Menai Straits ferry, from which the couple drew a considerable income. Five years after they were married, the Menai Suspension Bridge was opened and the couple were honoured guests at the opening ceremony when their carriage was 'drawn by four elegant greys, decorated with ribbons', so the *Chester Chronicle* reported. Sir David died in 1841 aged forty-eight, and was buried at Cambo. An obituary notice recalled: 'He made his tenantry comfortable and happy, gave them additional accommodation, and at his own expense drained their farms'.

John Evans, 1876–1931

John Evans lived at No. 2 Albert Place, Colwyn Bay. He was a brave fireman, one of only ten that Colwyn Bay had during the First World War. He served with the brigade for sixteen years, and when he died a fire engine was brought to Albert Place and his coffin was placed on it. His helmet, belt, axe and long-service medal were placed on the coffin, which had already been draped with the Union Jack. His body was then taken through Colwyn Bay on the fire engine, accompanied by twenty-one firemen who had come from all over North Wales, while a large crowd gathered to watch the mournful procession. He was buried in Bron-y-Nant Cemetery. When he and his wife, Daisy Jane, got married they lived over a stable in Ivy Street, but later moved to the small terraced house in Albert Place, where they brought up eight children. It must have been a real job to squeeze the whole family into the home! Eight years before he died, aged fifty-five, he attended the fire that destroyed the first Pier Pavilion. There was little he and his colleagues could do, and the following morning he was pictured standing among the twisted, mangled and still smoking ruins of the pavilion. On his gravestone, his wife arranged for the inscription, 'Worthy of everlasting love and remembrance'; a sentiment still visible today.

Sir David Erskine's home.

John Evan's coffin on the fire tender outside his house in Albert Place.

John Evans.

Sidney Colwyn Foulkes OBE, Freeman of the Borough, 1885–1971

Sidney Colwyn Foulkes' father, Tom, was a builder. He built St John's Methodist church, and it was in that church that Sidney was baptised. He went to school locally and then studied at the Liverpool School of Architecture under St Charles Reilly. During the First World War, he served in the Royal Naval Air Service, and then returned to Colwyn Bay where he opened his own architectural practice. His first office was in the converted Capel Cyntaf, a conversion that he had designed. The office was on the first floor and the Cosy Cinema was on the ground floor; his secretary, Audrey, used to listen to the films through the wall as she typed. It is now Matthews' hardware store. He designed the Llandudno war memorial in the 1920s, the Arcadia Cinema on Princes Drive (now demolished), the new wing and wards at Colwyn Bay Hospital, and the Costain Building and Memorial Hall at Rydal School. He designed his own new office and had it built on Pwllycrochan Avenue, procuring planning permission in the conservation area by naming it a 'studio' rather than an office. He designed the department store for his friend W. S. Wood (now Peacocks) at the top of Station Road, and Dando's shop round the corner on Abergele Road. He also designed a large home for Mr Wood at No. 6 Norton Road. He designed the entire Elwy Road Estate, which was visited by the American architect Frank Lloyd Wright, and the Heaton Place Estate, which is tucked away between Ebberston Road West and Digby Road. The Wren's Nest, a private house on Lansdowne Road, is his design and is a particular

Rydal School classroom block and Memorial Hall, designed by Mr Colwyn Foulkes.

delight, as is a cluster of his domestic houses on Norton Road (Corner Croft), Digby Road (Nos 3 and 5, Ilex House) and Y Bwthyn (No. 48 on Tan-y-Bryn Road). He lived and died at Cotswold, Brackley Avenue, Colwyn Bay.

W. S. Woods department store, designed by Sidney Colwyn Foulkes.

Ednyfed Fychan, *c.* 1170–1246

Ednyfed Fychan is probably the most consequential person to whom Colwyn Bay can lay claim. He ranked second only in importance to Llewelyn the Great, whose chief counsellor he became; he was Llewelyn's seneschal, steward or chief retainer. Over the years, the name Fychan, anglicised to Vaughan, has spread far and wide, and it was from him, by direct male descent, that the house of Tudor sprang. He was in charge of the area from Abergele to Conwy, and he owned Criccieth, and had estates on Anglesey. He killed three captains of Ranulph, Earl of Chester, when North Wales was invaded in 1210, but his chief importance was as an ambassador or statesman, and the part he played in shaping the policy of Gwynedd was substantial. In 1235, he made a pilgrimage to the Holy Land. Five years earlier he had bought the land of Rhos Fynach (the Marsh of the Monks), on which today stands the pub of that name, Rhos Point, and the children's play area. In all probability, Llys Euryn, on the lower spur of Bryn Euryn, was Ednyfed Fychan's home, and the arches of his private chapel can still be seen in the north wall of Llandrillo-yn-Rhos parish church.

Ednyfed Fychan's home on Bryn Euryn.

Gronw ap Heilyn, *c.* 1248–1289

Gronw ap Heilyn was the great-grandson of Ednyfed Fychan, and in many ways he was more influential than his forebear. He was trusted by both the Welsh prince, Llwelyn ap Gruffydd, for who he acted as emissary and counsellor, and the English King, Edward I. He was a warrior, statesman and friend to the royals, and lived somewhere near Llysfaen. He was bailiff of Rhos (the area over which his great-grandfather had held sway), and a King's Justice for North Wales. As a descendant of Ednyfed Fychan, he was allowed to hold his land in Rhos-on-Sea rent-free, and in return he had to protect the approaches to Snowdonia. In early 1278, he headed Prince Llewelyn's envoys when they journeyed to Windsor to arrange the marriage with Eleanor de Montfort, and thus also gained the trust of Edward I, for whom he became a negotiator. In 1281, after King Edward had lost some confidence in Gronw ap Heilyn because of his well-known support for the Welsh prince's ambitions, Gronw and his grandfather, Sir Tudor ap Ednyfed, were appointed the chief commissioners by Llewelyn to settle the peace between him and the King. After Llewelyn's death, he remained constant in his support of David and to the last, while in retirement in Llysfaen, he acted as the last Prince's seneschal or counsellor. Unfortunately, he had a long-running dispute with a local landowner, Robert de Crevequer, which undermined his good standing with the King and his followers. When the Madoc rebellion brought mayhem to Denbigh and Caernarvon, Gronw was found amongst the insurgents, and may well have been killed in battle. There is a reference, in a survey taken at the time, that his lands in Llysfaen and Rhos had been returned to the King because he 'died outside the law', or 'died against the peace and had forfeited his portion'.

Marjorie May Guy, 1910–1988

Marjorie Guy, with her mother Mrs Annie Guy and her sister Ethel Rose (always known as Queenie), arrived in Colwyn Bay in 1926. Her father, George, had already died in 1917, aged fifty-seven. He had owned a large factory in Wednesbury making tubes, and had been the first person to export bicycles to America. More unfortunately, his factory had been the first to receive a direct hit from a Zeppelin during the First World War. Marjorie, her mother and her sister, who was later to become the Guide Commissioner for Wales, all moved into a house on Lansdown Road specially designed for them by Sidney Colwyn Foulkes. Mrs Guy named it The Wren's Nest. In 1918, Marjorie wrote *Joe Doughty*, which was published by A & C Black. It was a spy story from the First World War, and was based in a boy's school. It sold well and, to her delight, earned Marjorie a little money and much recognition. In 1949, she published a more general story, which she called *When Carter Ruled* and was published by H. J. Drake. In 1988, Marjorie's niece moved into The Wren's Nest with her son, Roger, so Marjorie, never having married, moved out to live with the gardener in Old Colwyn. Ever the bohemian author to the end.

The Wren's Nest, home of Marjorie Guy.

Major John Lang Hammond MC, 1920–1944

Jack Hammond was twenty-four years old when he lost his life at the Battle of Imphal, India, in 1944. He was attached to the Royal Welch Fusiliers and the 1st Battalion 4th Prince of Wales' Own Gurkha Rifles. He had lived with his father, John Athorn Hammond, his mother, Elsie Whitworth Hammond, and his twin sister Peggy, at Ashford, Princess Drive, Rhos-on-Sea. He was educated at Colwyn Bay Grammar School, which is now known as Eirias High School, and received a BSc (Hons) from London University. He loved walking over the hills of North Wales, and a few years before his death he wrote an account (never published) of 'some walks, tours and climbs' with the title 'Through North Wales', in which he notes that from his bedroom window he could see 'the summit of Carnedd Llewelyn some thirteen miles away'. He started his account with words that can now be an epitaph for his short life: 'Like everything else this story must have a beginning, presumably it will have an end as well but what that end will be remains in the hands of Providence'. When the news of his death reached Rhos-on-Sea, the twenty-three-year-old Olive Roberts, the wife of his good friend Alan, went to Mr and Mrs Hammond's home to talk to them and offer her sympathy. Seventy years later, she could still remember standing outside the back door to the house and hearing the sound of Mr Hammond weeping uncontrollably from within. Olive recalled that Mr Hammond had been told that Jack died charging up a hill, leading his men from the front, urging them to follow him.

Major John Lang Hammond.

Sir Quinton Hazell MBE, CBE, 1920–1996

Sir Quinton Hazell founded the after-market car component company in Mochdre, which became famous all over the world. He was born in Deganwy and served his apprenticeship at Braids Bros Garage in Colwyn Bay, a business that was owned by friends of his father. He began his business in 1946, in a room over a garage on Conwy Road, Mochdre, with £1,000 capital and four workers. Ten years later, he was employing 800 people, due mainly to the fact that there was an inevitable shortage of car and truck components after the war. It was a brave commercial move to base such a company in Colwyn Bay, a long way from the traditional British manufacturing centre. He hit on the idea of selling motor components in a neat box, which contained all that was needed for a particular job – previously each part was sold separately in a greasy bit of paper. He came up with this idea during the Second World War – when he served in the army and had been rescued from the beaches of Dunkirk – when he saw how the Americans coded their own products, making them easier to use. Each of his boxes bore the Welsh dragon as a trademark, and as the dragon was a respected symbol in the Far East, where the parts were known as The Dragon Product, this stimulated enormous sales in that part of the world. In 1973, Burmah purchased the company for £56 million when Sir Quinton was employing 7,000 people worldwide. There are many hundreds of families in Colwyn Bay who owe their financial independence to the work he created for them and his vision in being able to loosen the cartel of the motor parts industry.

Sir Quinton Hazell.

William Hollywood, 1901–1982

Bill Hollywood was the founder and inspirational leader of the Colwyn Bay Friendship Club; he ran the club for twenty-six years. He was born in Ireland, in Bray near Dublin. His parents were diplomats who worked in the United States of America. Sadly, they both died in a car accident when Bill was eight years old, so he was moved to Belfast to be looked after by his aunt. He did well at school and then became a professional photographer with a studio in Belfast, but his main interest was in the scouting movement, and he formed the 37th Belfast Scout Group. In 1939, he joined an RASC unit and served in it for the duration of the war. At the end of the war in 1945, he married the sister of a Colwyn Bay scoutmaster and moved to Colwyn Bay, where he applied for the post of youth leader for the town. He was a 'hands on' type of man, eager and enthusiastic, traits that encouraged him, in 1946, to obtain the keys to an empty building in Douglas Road, which he set about turning into a youth club. He started by recruiting six boys off the street and offering them table tennis games, quizzes, sing-songs, walking and camping. Two years later, with the help of Miss Robinson, whose brother, a pilot, had been killed during the war, he started a girls section. The backbone of the Friendship Youth Club was the formation of the Scout Group and the Girl Guide Group. Bill Hollywood gave his time willingly and without thought of financial gain. He took the young people on holidays, the first being to Belfast to meet the members of his old scout troop, and eighteen boys crossed the Irish Sea for £6 for a two-week holiday. Sadly his marriage failed, so the Friendship Club

The old Friendship Club building from where Mr Hollywood did so much good.

became his life. His scout group became the largest in Wales and other troops from all over the country came to stay at the Douglas Road headquarters. He continued to work at the job he loved until he was seventy years old. He was never really recognised for his invaluable contribution to the town, but his memory lingers on in the countless men and women whom he helped and encouraged in life.

Alderman Ethel May Hovey JP, 1870–1953

Ethel Hovey was one of eleven children of the Revd George Henry Hovey and his wife, Frances. Her father was a local preacher, draper and house furnisher, who owned a large department store, and they all lived in Sheffield. Her father was a keen Methodist and sent her and her sister Rosa (1865–1932) to the new Penrhos Girls Methodist College in Colwyn Bay. In December 1894, Rosa was appointed the 'Lady Principal' of the college, and invited Ethel to become the bursar. Ethel became interested in local politics, and in 1926 was appointed the chairman of the Urban District Council, the first lady to hold this post. In the same year she officially opened the new post office on Princes Drive, which has been shut and empty now for ten years. On 14 July 1939, she also officially opened the Nant-y-Glyn Maternity Home, which was known by the Ministry of Food civil servants as the Swell Hotel during the Second World War. In 1946, she became the first peacetime mayor of Colwyn Bay, and again she was the first lady to hold the post. She was appointed an alderman, and was involved in the creation of the Heaton Place Trust and the building of the Heaton Place Estate in Rhos-on-Sea where she laid a foundation stone bearing her name on 23 April 1952. On her appointment as an alderman, five houses were built in Tan-yr-Allt Street, Mochdre: Nos 19–27 on the corner of the Tan-yr-Allt Street and Singleton Crescent.

Ethel May Hovey.

All five houses have the same coloured doors, and were originally built to house soldiers returning from the First World War. The mayoral chain, still worn by successive mayors to this day, was presented to the town by Miss Hovey. Both Ethel and Rosa were sympathetic to the suffragettes, but were careful not to display this enthusiasm too publicly as it could have damaged their standing within the town. However, Ethel was instrumental in having a fountain built in Queen's Gardens to acknowledge the work of the League of Women. On her eightieth birthday, she had a party at the Rhos Abbey Hotel. At the start of the party, she sat on a large chair outside the hotel at the bottom of the steps and allowed each guest two minutes to greet their hostess, while her secretary, Blanche Emily Hildred, held a stopwatch. She and her sister Rosa and their brother, Arthur Clement (1871–1952), along with her secretary, all lived at Gorse Hill, Hafodty Lane, Upper Colwyn Bay. Clement was a rather remote figure (and a little strange) who rode about Colwyn Bay on a horse. When Penrhos College was evacuated to Chatsworth House, Derbyshire, during the Second World War, Clement took up residence in the local village, Edensor, to help supervise the move from Colwyn Bay. When Ethel Hovey died in the coronation year, her body was taken by the 10.15 a.m. train from Colwyn Bay to Sheffield, where she was buried. Before the coffin was carried onto the train, a ceremony and short religious service were held on the station plaform.

Penrhos College (Hydropathic Establishment) in 1895.

Monica Howarth (Manikam Sumetra), 1930–1990

Manikam was born to Brahmin Hindus who were on a pilgrimage to a holy shrine in Mysore, India, at the time. Manikam was not well at birth and her parents stopped at the Holdsworth Memorial Hospital, where Methodist missionary Sister Ethel Tomkinson agreed to look after the child until her parents returned. They never returned. Sister Ethel nursed the child back to health and continued to look after her. The Brahmins are members of the priestly caste, and one of the local priests arrived at the hospital and asked to take Manikam so that she could perform Bharatanatyam, the devotional South Indian dance, at the local temple. Sister Ethel feared that this sort of life could lead to one of prostitution, so she decided to take the four-year-old Manikam to her own family in Colwyn Bay. The Tomkinson family owned the printing business and stationers on Penrhyn Road, which eventually became a Sheldons; the premises are now empty. Manikam became Monica, and she flourished in an atmosphere of love and security. She was present, as a small girl, at the laying of the foundation stone of Rhos-on-Sea Methodist church. In the 1920s, Monica would have been a rare sight in Colwyn Bay, but she never suffered from racial prejudice. She went on to have six children of her own, became a well-respected member of the local church, and never wished to trace her own Indian family. Her saviour, Sister Ethel, spent fifty years in India helping lepers and the destitute, work for which she received the MBE in 1963.

Monica, the smallest girl in the largest hat, at the laying of the foundation stone of Rhos-on-Sea Methodist church in 1922.

William Henry Hughes, *c.* 1872 – *c.* 1947

William Hughes, born in Henllan, was the headmaster for twenty-six years, beginning in 1911, of the Old Colwyn National School, built in 1888 on Green Hill. The amazing thing was, he was stone deaf. He never married and he could just about lip read, but when the children wanted to be understood they had to yell in his ear. Oddly enough, he could play the piano but could not hear it. When the children were instructed to accompany his playing with singing, they would invariably sing any tune but the correct one. He often sent some of the children shopping for him, and he used to send two brothers, Jack and Walter Price, to Mr D. O. Williams' shop on Church Walks (now demolished) for snuff. The children respected him because he was kind and used the cane sparingly, which was unusual for those days. However, in the Punishment Book for 14 October 1913, it is recorded, 'Elias Hughes (12) whistling in class – two strokes of the cane on hands'. Perhaps he could hear the high-pitched screech of a whistle. Forty-six years later, Elias became the mayor of the Borough of Colwyn Bay. On 26 March 1915, as a special treat, Hughes allowed all the pupils to walk around the corner to Abergele Road to witness the startling sight of the first tram trundling through the village. He also invited the local vicar of St Catherine's church to talk to the pupils, and before leaving the school, the vicar would always ask for three or four boys to weed his asparagus bed at the vicarage (now the Llys Madoc flats). The school eventually closed in 1980, forty-three years after Mr Hughes retired, and is now the Old Colwyn Community Centre.

Old Colwyn National School, *c.* 1912.

Revd William Hughes, 8 April 1856 – 28 January 1924

The Revd Hughes was born in Llanystumdwy – as was David Lloyd George six years later – and became the first minister of Tabernacl Welsh Baptist chapel on Abergele Road, Colwyn Bay. He was also the pastor of Calfaria Baptist chapel, Old Colwyn, and of Ebenezer chapel, Llanelian. He travelled to Africa three times as a missionary, and more controversially founded the Congo Institute on the corner of Nant-y-Glyn Road and Rosemary Avenue. He brought young African boys, mostly from the Congo, to the Institute to be educated and then returned to their homeland, where he hoped they would bring enlightenment and what he maintained were the benefits of Christianity. Two of the boys, Kinkasa and Nkanza, young teenagers, both died in Colwyn Bay and are both buried in Old Colwyn Cemetery on Llanelian Road. For a while, the Congo Institute was very successful, and the Revd Hughes, with the help of H. M. Stanley and King Leopold II of Belgium, was able to raise a good deal of local private funding. In the end, however, his idea and plans were thwarted by the periodical *John Bull*, the *News Of The World* of its day, which accused Revd Hughes of wrongdoing and sexual immorality. The magazine printed lurid headlines such as 'Black Baptist's Brown Baby', and pandering to the readers' assumed racism, 'English Ladies and Negroes'. The national Baptist organisation, through jealousy of his success, and the missionary establishment, who did not like his radical ideas, did not help him and perhaps foolishly, like Oscar Wilde had done a few years earlier when he sued the Marquess of Queensberry for slander, he sued *John Bull* for libel. In so

Revd William Hughes and the Congo Institute boys.

doing, like Oscar Wilde, he lost his case, there was more unpleasant publicity and the whole concept of the Congo Institute came tumbling down. He was also financially naïve, and in the end he faced bankruptcy proceedings. Eventually he ended up at the workhouse in Conway, and after his death he was buried in Old Colwyn Cemetery, not far from the graves of his two African students.

Robert Jackson, 1915–1969

Robert Jackson was the founder, first curator and inspiration behind the Colwyn Bay Zoo, now known as the Welsh Mountain Zoo. Some years ago, his wife Margaret was amused to receive a letter addressed to the 'creator' of the zoo. Jackson was born in Knutsford, the youngest of four children whose father was a shipping buyer with an interest in gardening. From an early age, Mr Jackson took a keen interest in animals and in later years, he was described by Edward Higham as 'a ferocious individualist'. In his teens he became interested in snakes, and took up breeding tropical fish as a hobby. He trained as a water gardener, and just before the Second World War he started a small business selling reptile equipment and building water gardens. During the war he became a farmer, a reserved occupation, and met his future wife when, as a Land Girl, her tractor and trailer turned over and he stopped to help her. In 1947, he was helping Gerald Durrell to find homes for all the animals that Durrell was bringing back from his expeditions, as well as running his own business selling tropical fish. In 1948, he set up a registered company, Robert Jackson Naturalist Ltd, and two years later, with the help of the Isles family who owned the Belle Vue land in Manchester, he opened small seasonal zoos at Swanage, Great Yarmouth, Skegness, New Brighton, the Marine Lake at Rhyl, beside the lido at Deganwy and at Eirias Park. In 1958, with George Cansdale, he set up his second company, Zoological Exhibitions Ltd. He had always wanted to open a fully fledged zoo, and looked at two sites locally: the Crow's Nest in the Sychnant Pass and Bryn Dinarth, the former estate of William Horton on Tan-y-Bryn Road, Rhos-on-Sea. In October 1960, he received a letter from Bill Barker, the Colwyn Borough Parks superintendent, and Jack Percival, chairman of the Borough Park Committee, inviting him to consider the Flagstaff Estate as a suitable place from which he could run his zoo. The deal with the council was done, and in November 1962 Mr and Mrs Jackson, along with their three young sons, Tony, aged sixteen, Chris, aged fourteen, and Nick, aged twelve, moved on to the site. The zoo was officially opened on 18 May 1963 and was quickly followed by one of the worst winters within living memory. Robert Jackson died six years later when he was struck by lightning while he was out enjoying one of his great passions – fishing. To this day, Chris and Nick are still very much involved in the day-to-day running of the zoo.

Robert Jackson with the mayor, Councillor W. H. Fox, on the day the zoo opened, 1963.

Hugh Madog Jones, 1909–1992

Hugh Jones was a nurseryman, florist and floral artist who worked from Bryn Awel Gardens, Dolwen Road, Old Colwyn. He was born in Llanelian, his first job being a handyman on the Coed Coch Estate in Dolwen when he was sixteen years old. He then became an apprentice at Plas Newydd on Anglesey and Bodnant in the Conwy Valley. He was a self-effacing man, who never sought personal acclaim. He worked out of a First World War Army hut from Kinmel Park Camp, Bodelwyddan, which he erected at Bryn Awel Gardens in 1924, and which he always referred to as his 'studio'. Inside the hut, hung on placards, was a treasure trove of the world's collected wisdom; thoughts and sayings, intermingled with books and boxes, racks and ribbons and flowers. In 1988, he was described by a journalist as 'one of the best half dozen or so [florists] in Great Britain', and by another, 'He is certainly a past master at floral work, one of the best in the country I would say.' He was helped all his married life by his wife Dilys (1912–1987); they had no children. Two of the notices in his hut announced to visitors: 'You can build a house, but a home must grow' and 'One of the hallmarks of a good man is his eagerness to train a successor'. His market garden and hut are now gone, and the land is covered by the Maes Madog and Rhodfa Sant Elian housing estate.

Above and below: Hugh Madog Jones outside his studio.

Margaret Lacey, 1910–1989

For many years, Margaret Lacey was the pre-eminent dance teacher in Colwyn Bay. For some time in the 1950s, she ran her dancing school from the back room of a house on Kings Road in the West End of Colwyn Bay, and then the Metropole Hotel in Colwyn Bay. She was a larger-than-life character with a deep, manly voice, large spectacles, and her hair tied back in a severe bun. Each year she produced a show featuring all her pupils, which was invariably produced in the Pier Pavilion, or in the St John's church theatre (designed by Sidney Colwyn Foulkes) on Cliff Gardens, Old Colwyn. Each year she held a raffle to raise funds for the dancing 'academy'. One year, a nine-year-old girl, Jennifer Roberts, won the raffle and was delighted to discover that the prize was an enormous box of chocolates. The following year, the ten-year-old Jennifer, having been bought a raffle ticket by her mother and, expecting to win again, was cautioned by her mother not to expect to win, and not to be disappointed when the result was announced. Her mother was bemused, and Jennifer delighted and excited, to hear Miss Lacey declare that she had won again. She raced up to the stage to receive her box of chocolates, only to discover that the prize that year was a brace of pheasants. In later life, after she stopped her teaching, Miss Lacey became great friends with the film directors Roy Boulting and John Schlesinger, both of whom gave her very small parts in their films. She appeared in over thirty films between 1957 and 1985. Her most famous role was as a seemingly innocent Christian schoolteacher who smuggled diamonds in

Wern, Miss Lacey's home.

the bible for the henchmen Mr Wint and Mr Kidd in the James Bond film *Diamonds Are For Ever*; her character was later found murdered and her body recovered from an Amsterdam canal. She played a sweet old lady on the top of a bus in *The Family Way* with Hayley Mills, and another old lady in *The Ruling Class* with Peter O'Toole, and a motherly figure in *Only Two Can Play* with Peter Sellers. She eventually retired to a lovely cottage, Wern, in Rowen, and died in Llandudno Hospital in 1989.

Revd Bilton Langstaff, *c.* 1867–1928

The Revd Langstaff was the headmaster of Rhos College on Abbey Road, Rhos-on-Sea, during the 1920s. In later years, the building was used by the Catholics as another school, St Mary's College. The college, a privately run school, had an excellent reputation and the Revd Langstaff was a typical product of his time; hard working, stern, benevolent, with a studied, little seen, sense of humour. He was known by the boys as 'The Gaffer'. One morning a pupil, Alan Roberts, breezed into the classroom flinging open the door and shouting, 'anyone seen the Gaffer?', upon which, from behind the blackboard, came the unmistakable voice answering 'Ad sum' (Latin for present). A chastened Alan was asked to 'see me later, outside my study'. There were five boys in the school with the surname Roberts, and they were known as Roberts Major, Roberts Minor, Roberts Tercius, Roberts Quartus, and Roberts Quintus. Trouble arose when the eldest Roberts left the school and the staff forgot this fact, whereupon the wrong boys stepped up to be recognised when the teachers called out the wrong Latin grade. One of the school boys, Jimmy Miller, went on to receive the Military Cross for his bravery during the Second World War. In 1928, the Revd Langstaff invited the sixth form boys to his family flat for tea. He noticed that the grandfather clock had stopped at 3.00 p.m. and amid much protesting from his wife, he got up, opened the case and started the pendulum swinging again. Exactly a week later, at 3.00 p.m., he died.

Jennifer Longford, 1930–2012

Jennifer Longford was the illegitimate daughter of Liberal Prime Minister David Lloyd George and his secretary and mistress, Frances Stevens. After Frances Stevens died in 1972, having eventually married the widower Lloyd George in 1943, Jennifer discovered a note written in 1929 by her mother to Lloyd George, saying that she felt that she was pregnant and would send him a covert message if that proved to be the case. After Jennifer's birth she had sent him a telegram saying, 'The parcel we were expecting has arrived.' At the time, Lloyd George was sixty-six years old, and Jennifer was brought up to refer to him as Taid (Grandfather). He lavished affection upon her, and in order to hide her parentage, her mother officially adopted her. She is connected to Colwyn Bay by becoming a pupil at Penrhos College at the start of the Second World War. When the school was evacuated to Chatsworth House, she caught pneumonia and was eventually moved to the supposedly more clement surroundings

Revd Langstaff, with Alan Roberts behind him, 1927.

Greenfield, Penrhos College, where Jennifer lived in 1939.

of Headington School in Oxford. Her father knew all about Penrhos College because on 15 September 1910, as Chancellor of the Exchequer, he had laid the foundation stone for Greenfield, which was originally built as the science block but in later years became a girl's boarding house, on Llannerch Road East. It was in Greenfield that his daughter eventually lived. In 1954, Jennifer began teaching at Tabora Girl's School in Tanganyika and married Michael Longford, who was the secretary to the governor, Lord Twining.

Robert Loraine, 1876–1935

On 10 August 1910, the first aeroplane to land in Wales, an Antoinette, came down unexpectedly on the Rhos-on-Sea Golf Links. The pilot, the thirty-four-year-old Robert Loraine, was attempting the first flight to Ireland. The aeroplane was a huge, kite-like affair, which seemed to be held together by innumerable wires, and Loraine was perched precariously in the midst of all this with his feet hanging down into space. He was not sure where he was, and had to be redirected by the excited crowd. Robert Loraine was born in Liscard, Cheshire, and was a successful London and Broadway stage actor and a soldier, who enjoyed a side career as a pioneer aviator, which brought him to Rhos-on-Sea. He had learnt to fly at the Bleriot school at Pau, France, and it was he who coined the word 'joystick' to describe aircraft stick controls. On the stage, he was particularly associated with the plays of George Bernard Shaw, but also took on many Shakespearean roles. For an actor, he was an unusual man. During the First

Mr Loraine's plane, 1910.

World War, he flew with the Royal Flying Corps, winning the MC and the DSO, and was seriously wounded twice. At the end of the war he was elevated to lieutenant-general. Twenty-five years after he had given the people of Rhos-on-Sea and Colwyn Bay something to remember, and shown them something they had never seen before and would possibly never see again, he died in London aged fifty-nine.

Madog ab Owain Gwynedd, *c.* 1150–1200

Over 300 years before Christopher Columbus' voyage to America, it is suggested that Prince Madog, in order to flee the internecine violence at home, sailed there with a small fleet of boats from the small harbour at Rhos-on-Sea. The harbour then existed beside what is now the Rhos-on-Sea Golf Course, and the prominent detached house, Odstone. After they landed at what is now West Florida on Mobile Bay, Alabama, Prince Madog returned to Rhos-on-Sea to recruit settlers. After gathering ten ships of men and women, he set sail a second time, never to return. Legend has it that eventually they all settled somewhere in the midwest of the Great Plains. Over the ensuing years, many early travellers crossing the vast expanse of North America reported meeting 'Welsh Indians'. In 1608, explorer Peter Wynne reported that the Monacan Indian's language resembled 'Welsh'. The Monacans were a tribe collectively referred to by the Algonquian Indians as 'Mandoag'. Today there is a memorial stone in the garden of Odstone commemorating the legend of Prince Madog, and noting that this was the spot from which he sailed. Prince Madog's father, Owain Gwynedd, was a real prince and is widely considered to be one of the greatest Welsh rulers of the Middle Ages.

Frank Madren, *c.* 1863 – *c.* 1928

Frank Madren's initials can still be seen to this day engraved into the upper stonework of two faces of the turret of Rhos View, above the date 1893, on the corner of Sea Bank Road and the Promenade (on the opposite corner to The Hotel Rothesay). Frank was the son of William Madren, a coach painter from Llanrhos, where he also ran the Mostyn Arms. William moved to Colwyn Bay and began to develop Penrhyn Road, where his son Frank obtained the position of postmaster. The post office in those days was in Penrhyn Road, and the words 'Post Office Chambers' can still be seen above the doorway at No. 24. Frank soon tired of being a postman and became a builder himself, living at Plas Maelgwyn on Bay View Road where he kept all his building materials. At this time, around 1868, new roads were being built and drainage was being installed by a contractor from Caernarvon named Mr Bugbird. One of these projects was the drainage outlet into the sea opposite, where the Cayley Promenade meets the West Promenade, and the Coffee Pot Kiosk now stands. This drainage outlet still exists, and the water can be seen gushing out of the sea wall into the sea. Frank Madren knew Mr Bugbird, and to help develop this bit of promenade he bought the land on the corner of Sea Bank Road, next to the Colbourne Hotel, which had been built in 1892 (the date

Frank and Ellen Madren in the centre, sons Harold and George on the right outside No. 76 Abergele Road.

The building that Frank Madren built, Rhos View.

is emblazoned on the building). He was an enterprising man, a local entrepreneur, and by 1898, in the same year that Winston Churchill fought at the Battle of Omdurman in the Sudan, he had bought what today is No. 76 Abergele Road. From there he ran the Maelgwyn (named after his home) Fish, Game & Poultry Stores, with his wife and sons, Harold and George. It is to the early pioneers in Colwyn Bay, unfettered by the myriad rules and regulations of the modern world, full of bravado and enthusiasm, that we owe so much, and who are sometimes remembered only by their initials high up on tall buildings.

Guilherme d'Oliveira Marques, *c.* 1887 – *c.* 1960

For some years, Guilherme d'Oliveira Marques lived at Dinglewood School, just off Lawson Road in Colwyn Bay, where Mr James Wood MA, JP, was the headmaster. The extraordinary feature of this boy's stay in Colwyn Bay is the fact that he had travelled all the way from Brazil to be educated here. His ship had arrived at Southampton in 1897, and then he travelled up to Colwyn Bay with his brother. It is a story that illustrates the lack of fear and the thirst for knowledge that existed in earlier days. Also at the school at the same time as this boy was the future composer, John Ireland. In later life, Guilherme d'Oliveira Marques became a prolific artist in London whose work was highly regarded and collected. Dinglewood School must have had an exceptionally good, possibly international, reputation. During the Second World War, the school

Dinglewood School, in later years called Tyn-y-Maes.

building and the Edelweiss Hotel next door, was requisitioned by the Ministry of Food, and the Bread Division was run from the site. The school limped on for a few years after the war, then became a guesthouse until Tyn-y-Maes was burnt down in 1953.

Dr William McKendrick, MD, DPH, Freeman of the Borough of Colwyn Bay, 1904–1984

Dr McKendrick, who lived at Owendale, Alexandra Road, Colwyn Bay, was the medical officer of health when the Charter of Incorporation was granted to the Municipal Borough of Colwyn Bay on 20 September 1934, and he held that position for many years thereafter. Each year he would go to the Grammar School and give every child a thorough medical check-up. In 1949, he formed what he called the 'Clinic Committee' where he examined babies and their mothers, a revolutionary idea at the time. He insisted that all the ladies – and they were all ladies, he had no men at the clinic – be injected against polio. Thirty years later, in recognition of the fulsome service that he had rendered to the local community, he was presented with the Honorary Freedom of the Borough on 18 March 1974. In part the citation read that he was honoured 'as an acknowledgement of the eminent and distinguished service he has rendered to the Borough of Colwyn Bay by his concern over many years for many sections of the life of the Borough; particularly in the care of the elderly residents in the Borough, and for the well-being of its people generally'. John Neal, the son of Johnny Neal, the local Borough Parks supervisor, remembers Dr McKendrick, a friend of his father, best because he 'seemed to have a blunt needle when it came to immunising me'.

Dr William McKenrick.

The twenty-fifth anniversary party of granting the charter to the Borough. Dr McKenrick is in the front row, second from the right.

Nurse Grace McPhail, *c.* 1875 – *c.* 1940

In the 1940s, I was born in St Andrew's Maternity Nursing Home on Watkin Avenue, Old Colwyn. The home was owned and run by Miss Johnson who, on the death of Nurse McPhail, had taken over Miss McPhail's nursing home, Coed Coch Cottage on Station Road, and relocated the business to Watkin Avenue. In the 1900s, Coed Coch Cottage had been owned by the Hon. Mrs E. S. Ward, and was situated in what the locals called 'The Jungle', because it was surrounded by trees and housed a large rookery. The name became even more appropriate when Nurse McPhail moved in because she kept several horses, dogs, cats and domestic fowl. She employed an odd job man, John Hugh Jones, who made black boot polish in the nursing home, which he sold for 1*d* and 2*d*. During the First World War, Nurse McPhail toured Old Colwyn in her canvas-covered pony and trap, collecting food and money to provide parcels for local young men who had been recruited by the army. Her pony was draped patriotically in a Union Jack, which no doubt would have been substituted by the Welsh flag ninety-eight years later, and pennants flew from each corner of what the locals referred to as her 'covered wagon'. After the war, she started a very successful scout group, and provided them with cowboy-style hats. She would sit in her rocking chair and, while knitting, give the boys talks on drill and etiquette. When Nurse McPhail died, all her domestic animals were killed, and after her successor, Miss Johnson, had moved to Watkin Avenue, the new owners of Coed Coch Cottage transformed it into a private house named Chadkirk. It was eventually demolished in 1975, but you can still see one wall of the old barn beside what is now known as Bodlondeb Gardens.

Nurse McPhail, left.

'The Jungle', site of the original St Andrew's Nursing Home, 1984. In 1848 it was known as Coed Coch Cottage.

Edgar Thomas Meredith, 1884–1974

No. 2 Wynn Avenue in Old Colwyn is called 'Scotia'. The word Scotia is worked ornately into the ironwork of the front gate. Scotia was the name of a White Star Line ship, on which the first owner of the house, Edgar Thomas Meredith, sailed. Mr Meredith was the founder of the Meredith & Bros Garage at Queens Garage, Abergele Road, Old Colwyn, which eventually became Meredith & Kirkham Ltd, the buildings of which were pulled down a few years ago to make way for the present Aldi food store. Mr Meredith had been due to take up a post as an engineer on the new White Star Line ship, *Titanic*. But in 1912, while sailing as an engineer on RMC *Cedric*, he was taken ashore in Australia for an emergency appendix operation and so missed his posting on *Titanic*, which would almost certainly have resulted in his death; of all the *Titanic*'s crew, the engineers suffered the heaviest casualties. This fortunate circumstance made him determined to join the half-steam, half-sail, wooden-built Dundee whaler, SS *Scotia*, which had been commissioned by the Board of Trade to act as an ice patrol to protect steamships crossing the North Atlantic in the wake of the *Titanic* disaster. Mr Meredith was the chief engineer on the very first ice patrol from March to August 1913 to monitor the ice regions of Greenland and Labrador, north of the region where the *Titanic* sank. The International Ice Patrol continues its work to this day. Edgar had first gone to sea when he was fifteen years old after leaving Mid Wales, where he had been born, and making his way alone to Liverpool, where he signed on as an apprentice engineer, a skill that he would eventually use to found his highly successful Old Colwyn business.

Scotia, Mr Meredith's home on Wynn Drive.

Dick Moore's business on the left, *c.* 1970.

Richard Henry (Dick) Moore, 14 November 1913 – 1 March 2002

Dick Moore, along with his wife Marion, was the proprietor and baker of Buckley's Café, Colwyn Bay. In 1955, he also built the lovely large house, Bryn Onnen, at No. 74 Pen-y-Bryn Road (which he christened High Bank), where he lived for many years with his wife and sons, Michael and Colin. At the time of his death, he still held the record for Hampshire County Cricket Club's highest individual score of 316, which he set at Bournemouth in July 1937 when he was twenty-three years old. He made all the runs in one day between 11.30 a.m. and 7.00 p.m., when he was the last man out. He first played for Hampshire after leaving Bournemouth Grammar School in August 1931, aged seventeen. Three years later, he was rated by Wisden as 'probably the most promising young amateur in English cricket'. In 1936, he was promoted to the captaincy of the club, and by the time the war broke out, he had scored 6,026 runs in 137 first-class games. He married Miss Buckley, whose family owned the bakery business, and moved to Colwyn Bay during the war, where he was put in charge of a POW camp in Llangwstenin. He ran the business until it finally closed in the 1980s, and the building was incorporated into the National Provincial Bank on Abergele Road. He continued to play cricket for Denbighshire and became the president of Colwyn Bay Cricket Club, an office he still held at the time of his death.

Captain Morgan ap John ap David, Sixteenth-Century Privateer

Rhos Fynach pub and restaurant was once the home of a pirate and buccaneer, Captain Morgan – this was not the Captain Sir Henry Morgan who roamed the Caribbean a hundred years later and captured Jamaica. In 1186, Llewelyn the Great had allowed the Cistercian Monks to build a small abbey, near what we today know as Rhos Point, and to create a fishing weir on the seashore. This area became known as Rhos Fynach; 'heath of the monks'. In 1230, Llewelyn passed the land on to Ednyfed Fychan, and sixty-eight years later the abbey moved to Maenan. In 1575, the land came into the ownership of Robert Dudley, the Earl of Leicester, a great favourite of Queen Elisabeth I. For 'services rendered against the enemies of Queen Elizabeth I', the Earl of Leicester passed the land of Rhos Fynach on to Captain Morgan as a gift. Captain Morgan was an outrageous pirate who became an extremely effective irritant to the Queen's foes. The Queen was not particularly bothered about the methods used by her loyal seafaring subject, and was happy that he should be given peaceful sanctuary in Llandrillo-yn-Rhos. Four hundred and thirteen years later, by which time the building was called Cegin-y-Mynach, it was nearly demolished because of its poor condition. It had been used as a café and then remained shut for seven years before Councillor Harriet Pearce Geary voiced the opinion that 'the council had a moral obligation to renovate the building'. And thus it came to pass that the home of a pirate and an immoral buccaneer became a successful pub and restaurant in the twenty-first century.

Above and below: Rhos Fynach, *c.* 1920.

Sir Dr John Henry Morris-Jones MC, DL, MP, JP, Freeman of the Borough of Colwyn Bay, 1884–1972

Sir Henry Morris-Jones practised as a family doctor for twenty years at Rhoslan Surgery on the corner of Marine Road and Conwy Road in Colwyn Bay. The surgery building was pulled down in the 1980s, and has been replaced by the Rhoslan flats. He founded the Colwyn Bay Medical Society, which gave doctors the opportunity to meet each other once a month to discuss the treatment of illnesses, and in 1927 he founded the Colwyn Bay Rotary Club, an institution that is still thriving today. He was also the chairman of the Colwyn Bay Urban District Council from 1923 to 1924. He was a local magistrate, and after his death his will revealed that he had bequeathed funds for the foundation of the Sir Henry Morris-Jones Trust, which was to help the Borough's young people under the age of nineteen with their future professions. He was born in Waunfawr and was educated at Menai Bridge Grammar School. In 1931, he married widower Leila Paget-Marsland; they never had children. He served as a medical officer with the 2nd Battalion of the Worcestershire Regiment during the First World War, when he was awarded the Military Cross. He entered Parliament in 1929 as the Liberal member for Denbigh, having beaten Capt. Alan Crosland Graham of Clwyd Hall, Ruthin, the political private secretary to Lord Balfour. In 1932, he was appointed as an

Sir Henry Morris-Jones, centre, shaking hands with Mr W. S. Wood at the opening of the department store on Station Road (now Peacocks).

Assistant Government Whip, and from 1935 to 1937, he was a Lord Commissioner of the Treasury. He became the treasurer of the Parliamentary Medical Group, a Trustee of the MPs Pensions Act Committee, and a member of the Parliamentary delegation participating in events to celebrate the 150th anniversary of the founding of Australia. Soon after its liberation in 1945, he was also appointed a member of the Parliamentary Delegation to Buchenwald concentration camp, a long, long way away, and a different world from Colwyn Bay.

Johnny E. Neal, 1900 – *c*. 1970

For many years, Johnny Neal was the Borough Council Parks manager, which for some reason seemed to cover entertainment in the town as well. In 1926, he and his wife, May Berry, who became as well known locally as her husband through her dancing academy, opened a tea garden at Tan-y-Coed on Beach Road, Old Colwyn. In those days, most of the visitors to the town simply left their digs in the morning and went to the beach, returning for lunch and then once again heading for the beach for the afternoon, having to pass the tea gardens on their way. Neal had played football for Llandudno Football Club, and then transferred to the Colwyn Bay Club. He became a junior international, and in 1920 he set a North Wales record by scoring 137 goals

Tan-y-Coed Tea Gardens, owned by Johnny Neal and May Berry, 1930.

in one season. He played for Wales as a professional, and in the 1929/30 season, he was a member of the unbeaten Welsh team that toured Canada. As the parks manager for the town, he was much involved in the development of Eirias Park and the sports arena. During the war, when the Ministry of Food was located in the town, he was the 'Emergency Feeding Officer', responsible for running the British Restaurant. He was also the chief air-raid warden, and the liaison officer between the army and the civil defence, as well as allowing eleven American soldiers to stay in Tan-y-Coed until they left for the D-Day landings. In the 1950s, as the town's entertainment manager, he had to reprimand Tom, the young man who drove the mechanical elephant, because Tom was discovered, without a driving licence, leading the elephant through the town while ferrying one of the visitors to her holiday digs. Tan-y-Coed was demolished in 1974, and flats for the elderly now occupy the site.

Ian Niall, 7 November 1916 – 24 June 2002

Ian Niall was the pen name of John McNeillie, who was born in Wigtownshire in Scotland and became one of Britain's best-loved rural writers. During the Second World War he came to Old Colwyn, where he worked at the Ratcliffe Tool Company and lived at Thornfield, Coed Coch Road (now No. 76, and still called Thornfield to this day). He lived in North Wales for the rest of his life. Wales and the Welsh provided the background for many of his books, although when he was twenty-two years old, he caused a furore by publishing *Wigtown Ploughman: Part of His Life*, which was a fictional account of the impoverished lives of the local people. For some prejudiced people, this was 'proof' that their view about the 'immorality' of the cotters in the Machars of Wigtownshire was correct. The book played a key part in the instigation of housing reforms in the region. Once he arrived in Colwyn Bay, aged twenty-three, with a reclusive and self-effacing nature, he wrote prodigiously for *Country Life* and *The Spectator*. However, he never made much attempt to promote himself or his work. In 1950, he wrote *The Poacher's Handbook*; in 1961, *Trout From The Hills*; and in 1971, a novel – *The Village Policeman* – about a man's life in Meirionydd, based on the family papers of Anglesey policeman Kenneth Williams. He also wrote a novel called *The Deluge* about the 1952 Dolgarrog dam disaster. From his work, readers became familiar with countryside lore, from retrieving ferrets from deep burrows to reading the cries of flushed magpies. He wrote a biography of the bird illustrator C. F. Tunnicliffe, and as a keen fly fisherman, wrote regularly for the monthly magazine *Angling*. His life and thought were influenced by the time he spent as a child with his paternal grandparents on a remote North Clutag farm, around which the Eden of the horse-drawn world of Robert Burns still lingered. This formed the backdrop to almost all he wrote.

Coed Coch Road where Mr Niall lived and worked during the Second World War.

Mr Niall's house, second from right, Coed Coch Road.

Herbert Luck North, 1871–1941

Herbert Luck North was an architect much influenced by the Arts and Crafts movement, who, due to family associations, came to live and work in North Wales at Llanfairfechan. Unconventionally, he worked from a bedroom in his own home, Wern Isaf, which he had designed himself. His clients in Colwyn Bay were not overtly wealthy or architecturally sophisticated, so his houses in town are relatively small. Nevertheless, they are distinguished and identifiably by North, with the later help of his partner, P. M. Padmore. It is said that he was temperamentally old-fashioned – a man who understood the need for progress but whose heart was aesthetically bound by tradition. And therein lay his appeal, and his historical stamp on our town. He designed two houses in Trillo Avenue in Rhos-on-Sea, Nos 4 and 6; two on Ael-y-Bryn Road, Colwyn Bay (Nos 4 and 6); the Highlands, originally called Penwartha, on Hafodty Lane, Upper Colwyn Bay; and three homes – Halfryn, Ty Gwyn and Wyniat – on Minffordd Road, Llanddulas. North's style of architecture was not necessarily 'Welsh' by tradition, but his homes sit well in their surroundings, are well-built and full of character; they are not bland. Once you have seen a house designed by Herbert Luck North, you will readily recognise his style whenever you see it elsewhere and rejoice.

Highlands, designed by Mr North.

Thomas George Osborn, 1843–1910

Thomas Osborn, a long-standing Methodist and always known as TGO, was the founder of Rydal School. In May 1885, by which time he had seven children, he advertised the fact that he was opening a boy's boarding school in Colwyn Bay. He had been a very successful headmaster of Kingswood School, Bath, but with the help and financial backing of Revd Frederick W. Payne, who at the time of the school's opening was the superintendent of the North Wales Coast Mission, he started the school in Colwyn Bay. He knew Colwyn Bay because his daughter was one of the first pupils of the fledgling Penrhos College – Revd Payne being the force behind its foundation. In 1883, Revd Payne built a home for himself on the corner of Lansdowne Road and Pwllycrochan Avenue, which he named Rydal Mount. He sold this house to Mr Osborn, from which the school, still situated there, took its name. He started the school with two unqualified masters and fourteen pupils, one of whom was his own son, and another of whom was the son of a governor of the school. By 1899, the number of pupils had risen to 109. Mr Osborn died in April 1910, and for the next five years his son, unsuccessfully, took over the running of the school, until the second year of the First World War. The Revd A. J. Costain then took over and ushered in a new dawn of enlightened success.

Rydal School during Mr Osborn's day.

Alderman Revd Thomas Parry JP, Freeman of Colwyn Bay, 1842–1936

The Revd Parry, a self-taught architect, was born in Llangernyw. His father died when Thomas was one year old, and his mother died when he was aged three. It was he who did more than anyone to develop Colwyn Bay towards the end of the nineteenth century, building many of the first houses in Colwyn Bay, and some of the chapels. He was the first chairman of the Urban District Council of Colwyn Bay, and was the first person to receive the freedom of Colwyn Bay, at ninety-three years old. When he first arrived in the town, the old turnpike road was worn; it was dangerous to pedestrians and destructive to carts. He was quoted as saying, 'it was very dangerous for children who had to walk from Eirias Bridge to the Board School, amongst carts and carriages without anywhere to run for safety.' He resolved to improve it. Incredibly, his efforts were met with opposition on the grounds that the scheme would cost money. Nothing changes! From 1881 to 1897, he was chairman of the Llandrillo-yn-Rhos and Eirias School Board, and became the chairman of the Cottage Hospital, the free library and Denbighshire County Council. He began his building career as Abel Roberts' foreman at Mr Roberts' workshop in Ivy Street. In 1872, Revd Parry sailed to America, where he preached at Alliance in Ohio. However, he hankered for his Welsh homeland and returned and set up his own building business behind Engedi Chapel. He built his own home, Llys Aled, on the corner of

Above and next page: Hermon Chapel (now demolished) designed and built by Revd Thomas Parry.

Woodland Park and Coed Pella Road, which still stands today. He built Hermon Chapel on Brompton Avenue, where Capel-yn-Rhos stands today. He designed and built Hebron Chapel, Bodelwyddan Avenue, Old Colwyn, and Shiloh Chapel on Greenfield Road, which is now used by Coastal Ceramics, a kitchen and bathroom business. His company built Calfaria Chapel on Princes Road, Old Colwyn, all the buildings in Colwyn Bay on Conwy Road between Hawarden Road and Penrhyn Road; and the large house, The Towers, which stands on the corner of York Road and Woodland Park. His wife, Mary, died twenty-six years before he passed away, and they now lie together in Llandrillo-yn-Rhos parish churchyard.

Madame Adelina Maria Clorinda Patti, Baroness Cederstrom, 19 February 1843 – 27 September 1919

Adelina Patti was born in Madrid, and was possibly the most famous opera singer of the nineteenth century, earning huge fees at the height of her career in the music capitals of Europe and America. It was therefore greatly to his credit and a real coup that Monsieur Jules Rivière, the musical director of the newly built Colwyn Bay Pier Pavilion, was able to secure her services at the opening ceremony of the pavilion on 2 June 1900. She was like a rock star of her day. She was enormously popular and remains one of the most famous sopranos in history due to the purity and beauty of her lyrical voice. She also invested the word 'diva' with a special resonance; she had a repertoire of dirty tricks to sabotage the singing of whoever shared a stage with her. The day after the official civic opening of the pier itself, Madame Patti was given a civic reception at the railway station, where she walked on a new red carpet purchased especially for the occasion. The chairman of the Council, George Bevan JP, presented her with an illuminated album in sage green, containing fourteen photographs of the local scenery. She was then driven to the Pavilion, passing beneath a huge banner that read, 'Welcome To The Queen of Song'. It was well known that she possessed girlish good looks, which gave her an appealing stage presence and added to her celebrity status, and the Colwyn Bay crowd were eager to witness this for themselves. Many in the crowd were finding it difficult to see this apparition, and there were shouts of 'Pull down the hood'. This was done and she and her husband continued at a stately pace, greeted at the Pavilion by a packed and expectant audience. She sang Gounod's 'Jewel Song' from *Faust*, followed by further songs in Italian, and ended with the song with which she was primarily associated, 'Home Sweet Home', a song which she had sung at the White House for the President of the United States, Abraham Lincoln, and his wife. Adelina Patti's career was one of success after success; she sang in Russia, South America, Spain, Italy, and Colwyn Bay. In her prime, Madame Patti was paid $5,000 a night! Mercifully there are no records of what she was paid when she came to Colwyn Bay.

The Colwyn Bay Pier Pavilion in Madame Patti's day.

Adelina Patti.

Revd Frederick Payne, 1814–1895

In 1864, the Revd Payne arrived in Llandudno to take charge of the small English Wesleyan Methodist chapel in the town, and so began a thirty-year ministry in North Wales. He was an ambitious man who pushed through enlightened ecclesiastical building projects. He was helped in this endeavour by a special fund, raised by a well-known minister of the time, the Revd W. Morley Punshon. Sadly, his only son died in a tragic climbing accident in 1873, which only seemed to spur him on in his work. By 1881, he had his eye on Colwyn Bay, which had become an increasingly popular resort and residential area, and which was to become, with his help, an educational centre. He became the honorary secretary of the Methodist Boarding Schools Association. This association was instrumental in the foundation of Penrhos College in 1880, which started its life in a large house called Gilbertville on the corner of Penrhos Avenue and the Promenade. At the time, after the death of Sir David Erskine, the Pwllycrochan Estate was being broken up, and the Revd Payne bought two parcels of land, one for a church and manse and one for himself, intending to build a house in which to end his days. In August 1882, on the plot of land on the corner of Conwy Road and Pwllycrochan Avenue, a stone-laying ceremony was performed, and within a year a church schoolroom and large manse (now a nursing home) were built on the land. The money then ran out and the area became known locally as 'Wesley's Folly'. Five years later, during Queen Victoria's Golden Jubilee celebrations, he was able

Wesley's Folly (St John's church) completed.

to complete St John's Methodist church, with the builder Tom Foulkes. He built his own home, which he named Rydal Mount, on the corner of Lansdown Road and Pwllycrochan Avenue. He sold this in 1885 to George Osborn, who was the first headmaster and founder of Rydal School. He also built an enormous house, Beechholme (now a Rydal-Penrhos School boarding house), further up the Avenue on the corner of Combermere Road, in which he intended to spend his retirement. Unfortunately, his health deteriorated and in his last years he went to live with his daughter, who also lived in Colwyn Bay.

Lady Maria Peacock, 1874 – c. 1956

Maria Peacock (*née* Timmins) was the second wife of Sir Peter Peacock JP, the six times mayor of Warrington and a freeman of the town. Sir Peter's first wife had been Maria's older sister who died, aged nineteen, while giving birth to a son. Maria began to look after the baby and subsequently married the baby's father. She and Sir Peter Peacock went on to become the parents of six further children; five boys and one girl. In later life the girl, Marion, became a well-respected elocution teacher at Penrhos Junior School, and a Liberal councillor with Colwyn Bay Borough Council. There is family testimony to support the notion that Maria Peacock had a bad temper, throwing the occasional tantrum and refusing to show up at civic functions. Sir Peter eventually got fed up with this behaviour and went to live in Birmingham with Letitia Rose Tynan, a postal worker. A product of this union

Kensington Avenue.

was the birth of Kenneth Tynan, the future drama critic, journalist and architect of Laurence Olivier's National Theatre repertoire. The rejected Maria, still the official wife of Sir Peter, came to live in Wales, ending up at No. 21 Kensington Avenue, Old Colwyn, where she remained up until her death. On the wall of the hallway of the semi-detached house hung an enormous painting of Sir Peter Peacock in his red mayoral robes. When Sir Peter died, he was buried anonymously in the same grave as his first wife. Maria would not give her permission for a headstone to be erected on the plot. After Maria's death, her maid and housekeeper, Alice Galloway, who had been with her employer since Sir Peter's defection to Rose Tynan, remained in the house for many years.

John Merry Porter, 1863–1942

Sir David Erskine died in 1841, and when, in 1865, his son Sir Thomas Erskine and widow, the Dowager Lady Erskine, put the Pwllycrochan Estate up for sale, John Pender, a Manchester businessman, bought the entire estate. The following year his agent, John Porter, bought the Pwllycrochan mansion, the Erskine's former home, and ran it as a very superior and successful hotel. It remained the property of the Porter family until 1938, when it was sold to Rydal School. His son, John Merry Porter, went to school in Conway and was then articled to Messrs Farrer & Co. of Manchester, where he trained as an architect and surveyor. He qualified in 1886, returned to Colwyn Bay and formed a partnership with Lawrence Booth and Thomas Chadwick, and acted as agents for the Colwyn Bay and Pwllycrochan Estate Company, and also ran the family Pwllycrochan Hotel business. This business, known as J. M. Porter & Co., was run from No. 37 Conwy Road and the words, 'Estate Office' can be seen to this day inscribed into the stonework at the top of the building. The firm remained in operation until its dissolution in 1973. In 1891, Mr Porter married Catherine Hawksworth at St Paul's church; they had three children, but the eldest, Graham, was killed in action in France in 1916. He built a house for his family on Pen-y-Bryn Road, which he named Braeside, and which later became the clubhouse for Colwyn Bay Golf Course, now the site of the Pen-y-Bryn pub and restaurant. He became a magistrate in 1914, and was chairman of the County Council in 1920. He was also a founder member of the St Trillo Lodge of Freemasons.

John Merry Porter.

Captain Thomas Price JP, High Sheriff of Denbighshire, *c.* 1560 – *c.* 1629

Captain Price was an Elizabethan seadog. He was a poet, soldier, seaman and explorer, and is believed to be, along with Captain Will Myddelton, the first person to smoke tobacco publicly in Wales, having captured a cargo of the stuff from a Spanish ship off the Canary Islands. He was appointed a treasurer, to cover what we now know as Colwyn Bay, to levy, collect and distribute money towards the relief of maimed soldiers. His headquarters, from where he carried out this task, was at Groes-yn-Eirias, the birthplace of Blessed William Davies (see page 35), where today the main gates of Eirias Park stand opposite the bottom of Groes Road. In 1601, at Groes-yn-Eirias, when Captain Price was attempting to extract money from the local people, there was an inn, a cross, possibly where the mini roundabout is now situated, and Groes farm. He was an unpopular man, as taxmen have traditionally been, and while he was trying to cross the River Conway by ferry, he was confronted by an unruly mob with 'swords, daggers, long staffs and picks', who were fortunately dissuaded from using this arsenal by 'some well-disposed persons'.

Mr Greenwood's smithy at Groes-yn-Eirias, *c.* 1914.

Professor John Raeburn, 1912–2006

John Raeburn spent five years in Colwyn Bay during the Second World War, and was responsible in one very important way for the survival of the British people. He had been born in Aberdeen, but went to Manchester Grammar School after his father moved to that city. Crucially, he had been a farm labourer before attending Edinburgh University. Three years before the war began, he was appointed the professor of Agricultural Economics at Nanking. On the outbreak of war, he joined the Ministry of Food as a statistician, and in 1941, he became the head of the Agricultural Plans Division. He carried out all this work in Colwyn Bay, where the Ministry of Food was based during the war. He met his wife Mair, a nurse, while he was in Colwyn Bay, and they were married in the town in 1941. His most important role while stationed in Colwyn Bay was to originate, front and organise one of the great wartime home front success stories; the 'Dig for Victory' campaign, which was instrumental in feeding the British people. Gardens, lawns and golf courses were dug up to provide vegetables. City dwellers as well as country folk took to keeping chickens, rabbits and goats. Pigs were popular because they thrived on household waste. Characters such as Dr Carrot and Potato Pete extolled the masses to even greater efforts. When there was a glut of carrots, the beneficial effects of carotene on eyesight, or helping people to see in the black-out, were promoted and soon helped to clear the mountain of carrots. In 1944, from the Colwyn Bay Hotel, he issued a prescient warning: 'even if it [the war] were to end in Europe sooner than we expect, the food situation, far from becoming easier, may well become more difficult owing to the urgent necessity of feeding the starving people of Europe. Indeed in many ways it would be true to say that our real tasks will only then begin. Carry on therefore with your good work.' Professor Raeburn had a great thirst for travel, and after the war he indulged himself in this wanderlust. He was on the Colonial Economic Research Committee (1949–1961), a member of the UN agricultural mission to Yugoslavia in 1951, and a consultant to the World Bank (1979–1988), and every now and again he would return to Colwyn Bay.

Flight Lieutenant Ronald (Ron) Rayner DFC, 1921–1999

Ron was born in Manchester but came to live in Rhos-on-Sea after the Second World War because, during the war, his parents had been bombed out of their home and had come to live on Everard Road, where they ran a boarding house. Ron's wife Midge had also come to Rhos to be with Ron's parents, so Ron inevitably followed them. After the war, he worked in Beardsall's jeweller's shop on Penrhyn Avenue, running the jewellery and photographic side of the business while Eddie Beardsall concentrated on the optician part. During the war he flew Spitfires. On one occasion, he flew his plane in a searchlight co-operation exercise, during which he was easily detected because he forgot to switch off his navigation lights! On another occasion, his plane was badly damaged when his squadron was over St Omer in France attempting to entice the German fighter aircraft to come up and attack them. He managed to land, although his canopy had been shot away and dust from the perspex had got into his oxygen mask. He was at Tangmere aerodrome, and was commanded by Wing Commander Douglas Bader. Ron was on the bombing raid as an escort Spitfire when Bader's artificial legs were dropped over Germany because Bader had been captured and left his original pair in his burning aircraft. Ron flew missions when the allied forces landed in North Africa, Malta, Sicily and, most heroically of all, at Salerno, where he shot down and killed Kommodore Hauptman Wiglav von Wedal. During a strafing sortie over Northern Italy, he had a narrow escape when a shell went up through his Spitfire's wing root – just 3 feet from his seat. Ron very rarely spoke about any of this, for he was a modest and self-effacing man.

Flight Lieutenant Ron 'Cloudy' Rayner DFC.

King Richard II, 6 January 1367 – 14 February 1400

In 1399, King Richard II was ambushed in Colwyn Bay by his enemies and subsequently died. He was born on the feast of Epiphany at the Abbey of St Andrew in Bordeaux, in the English principality of Aquitaine. It is believed that three Kings were present at his birth: the King of Castille, the King of Navarre and the King of Portugal. He became King when he was ten years old, and the country was run by a series of councils. In 1381, he helped to suppress the Peasants' Revolt, but six years later a group of discontented noblemen took over the running of the country. In 1397, he took his revenge on these people, many of whom he either executed or exiled, and for the next two years he ruled on the basis of the fear he engendered in his countrymen. It is now believed that his policies were not unprecedented or entirely unrealistic, but the way in which he carried them out was wrong and this led to his downfall and capture in Colwyn Bay. He had foolishly disinherited and exiled his cousin, Henry of Bolingbroke, who in June 1399 returned to Britain intending to claim the throne for himself. At the time, King Richard was in Ireland, but on hearing about Bolingbroke's return, he hurried back to the mainland with a small retinue and stayed overnight in Conwy Castle. He had expected his army to be waiting for him but it had dispersed. Bolingbroke was at Chester and his chief supporter, Henry Percy, Earl of Northumberland, went to Conwy to meet the King, whereupon he deceived his monarch by swearing on the holy relics on the altar of Conwy Castle's garrison chapel that the King would be safe, and persuaded him to follow him to Rhuddlan. The Earl of Northumberland had arranged for his men to be waiting at Penmaen Head, and when the King and his men tried to negotiate the headland they were surrounded and held captive. Four hundred and fifty years before the trainline was built around the headland, and 570 years before the A55 was constructed, they had no means of escape. It was reported that, 'Then did the King demean himself so sorrowfully, that it was a pity to behold.'

Thomas James Richardson, 1889–1950

Rich, as he was known to his friends, was a Colwyn Bay hairdresser who worked from his shop at No. 6 Belgrave Road. Ten years after selling his business and leaving the town, he stood beside Stalin, Winston Churchill and Franklin Roosevelt in the Crimea as they decided the future of the world and of the lives of millions of people. His father, James, was an Irishman from Lisburn, who made a living as a carpenter and who had worked on the building of the *Titanic*. He also did sculpture work on a church in Southport because the Italian craftsmen were afraid to travel to England by sea. Sadly, he drank too much and was cruel to Rich and his seven siblings, so his wife shooed him off, after beating him with her sweeping brush, back to Ireland where he remained. When Rich left Colwyn Bay, he became the chief barber on board the Cunard White Line ships, the *Queen Mary*, sailing on its maiden voyage, and the *Queen Elizabeth*. During the 1930s, he was paying £1,000 per year for the concession to run the *Queen Mary*'s salon. He became a friend of the Duke and Duchess of Windsor, who always

Penmaenhead where Richard II was captured.

The property with the low roof is where Rich's hairdressing business was located.

insisted that he do their hair. He also cut the hair of Ivor Novello, Jack Dempsey, Gracie Fields, Marlene Dietrich and Douglas Fairbanks. During the Second World War, he remained on the *Queen Mary* when it was used as a speedy troop ship. However in February 1945, he accompanied Winston Churchill to the Yalta Conference as he resembled the war leader and was asked to dress in an identical way to Churchill to confuse any potential assassins. He is standing just out of range of the camera in the famous photograph of the war leaders and their advisors as they take a break from their negotiations. Rich continued to work on the *Queen Mary* until the day he died. Two of Mr Richardson's brothers spent all their lives in Colwyn Bay and finished up living in the Constitutional Club. All three of his sisters married and also stayed in the town.

Jules Prudence Rivière, 1819–1900

Jules Rivière was born in Aix-en-Othe, France, and died in Colwyn Bay, where he is buried in Llandrillo-yn-Rhos parish churchyard. On his headstone are engraved the words: 'Music, when soft voices die, vibrates in the memory.' Rivieres Avenue in Colwyn Bay was named in his memory, as was the west window in St Trillo church. He had

VICTORIA PIER & PAVILION COMPANY
(COLWYN BAY), LTD.
Manager and Secretary   -   -   -   -   Mr. FRED V. BURGESS.

Concerts Daily
AT
11 a.m. & 7-45 p.m.

Sundays (Sacred) 8-15 p.m.

Riviere's
Grand Orchestra,

arrived in London in 1857, having been the bandmaster of the 12th Regiment of Light Infantry, and the conductor at Le Jardin d'Hiver on the Champs-Elysées. In his first hotel in London, his sleep was interrupted by a family of acrobats who practised their somersaults in the room above. By 1866, he was the director of the opera and ballet at the Alhambra in London, and in the 1870s his Promenade Concerts had become very popular. In 1887, he became the musical director for the Llandudno Pier Pavilion, but three years later his relationship with the pier directors had soured to such an extent that he moved his whole orchestra to the Victoria Pier Pavilion at Colwyn Bay. He was very popular and proved a wonderful attraction. Sadly, he died fairly soon after setting up his orchestra on the pier. Twenty years previously, he had married a twenty-one-year-old English girl from Bath, Amy Frances Fisher. She died thirty years after her husband, and is buried alongside him in Llandrillo-yn-Rhos parish churchyard.

Alan Noel Roberts, 1909–1991

The unsung hero and best social worker of many communities is often the funeral director. This was never more true than of Alan Roberts. His grandfather, Jessie Roberts, was born in Trofarth, Bryn-y-Maen, and in 1856 he walked all the way to Harpurhey, Manchester, to look for work. He became a carpenter before starting to arrange funerals, and in 1894 asked his son, Percy, to join him at work. Percy eventually retired to Rhos-on-Sea with his wife and young son Alan. Alan was born on Christmas Day, hence his middle name. He could recall that when he was six years old, in 1915, he went with his father to see Buffalo Bill, Annie Oakley and Chief Sitting Bull at the Wild West Show at Belle Vue, Manchester. After the family had arrived in Rhos-on-Sea, people heard about Percy's profession and started asking him to arrange their relative's funerals, and Alan, at first reluctantly, was drawn into the business. In 1940, a few days after the army had been saved from the beaches of Dunkirk, he married Olive Gatley, an eighteen-year-old local girl, and they subsequently had four children. When T. Conchar & Sons, a long-established funeral company in Colwyn Bay, was put up for sale in the 1960s, Alan bought the business. As necessity dictates in the world of funerals, Alan worked long hours and every day, including his birthday and New Year's Day. He was a popular, humorous man, a good listener and dedicated to helping people at a traumatic time in their lives. He ended up arranging, on average, 500 funerals each year, and so got to know more people in the town and the intricacies of their lives than possibly anyone else, certainly more than any town councillor or doctor. He was a lovely, compassionate man for whom I had great affection. He was my father.

Alan Noel Roberts.

Edward Meirion Roberts, 17 May 1913 – November 1995

Meirion Roberts was an exceptionally gifted graphic designer, artist and cartoonist. He was born in Llan Ffestiniog, and moved to Colwyn Bay in 1955. He lived with his wife, Eirwen, and children at Trefin, Min-y-Don Road, Old Colwyn. He worked for and eventually became a director of the McConnell Advertising Company based on Princes Drive. As an eleven-year-old boy, he contracted osteomyelites, which necessitated him enduring twenty-six operations and living in Denbigh Infirmary for two years. It was during those years that he began to paint and draw. When he resumed his schooling, he was so far behind that he found he was unable to make up ground and left school when he was fifteen years old. He eventually found work in a garage in Bala, earning 7/6p a week, but when he was sixteen he was sacked and replaced by a younger boy on a lower wage. His mother encouraged his artistic ambitions, and he went to Westminster Art School in Chester for two years on a grant of £25 a year, which had to be repaid by his parents. He then went looking for work in London, where he found his first job with Amalgamated Artists in Shoe Lane, who paid him £1 2s 6d a week, and where he worked on an instruction leaflet for a lifeboat, parts of which had been designed by Lawrence of Arabia. When war came he signed up as a despatch rider and found himself in Egypt, where he painted the Roman Temple of Baalbeck and produced paintings for the Officer's Mess, many of which were purloined by the officers and brought back to Britain to decorate their own homes. After returning home, he drew his first Eisteddfod Declaration Scroll, which was in use for fifty years, and in 1948 he designed the first illustrated cover for the Llangollen International Eisteddfod programme. The first full-page colour advert to appear in a British newspaper, of a Vauxhall VX490, was one of his designs. He designed some 600 book jackets and worked on projects for John Player, Bass Brewery and Shell Oil, but he is best remembered for the £500,000 he raised for the National and Urdd Eisteddffodau by producing his Eisteddfod maps, which were highly sought after and immediately became collectors' items.

Robert Evan Wynne Rowlands, 1890–1973

Robert Rowlands was a tailor and lived his whole life in Mochdre. He married Lucy, who was his staunch supporter through thick and thin for their entire married life. They went to live at Bryn Derfel, a small, low-lying terraced house, in Chapel Street, Mochdre, and it was from there that he carried out his one-man business. He always sat cross-legged on his work bench, the top of the table in the front room, surrounded by snippets of cloth – just as Beatrix Potter describes in *The Tailor of Gloucester* – while he mended the clothes, which were brought to him from across the local district. He enjoyed taking snuff, and the area below his nostrils was tanned brown from his lifelong use of the stuff. Each year he attended the Llangollen Eisteddfod, and in June 1949 he was pictured in the local paper with two Irish Colleens on either arm, and every year he took some part in the Mochdre May Day Parade. Sometimes the local boys, including Peter Rawlings, a future highly respected Colwyn Bay chartered

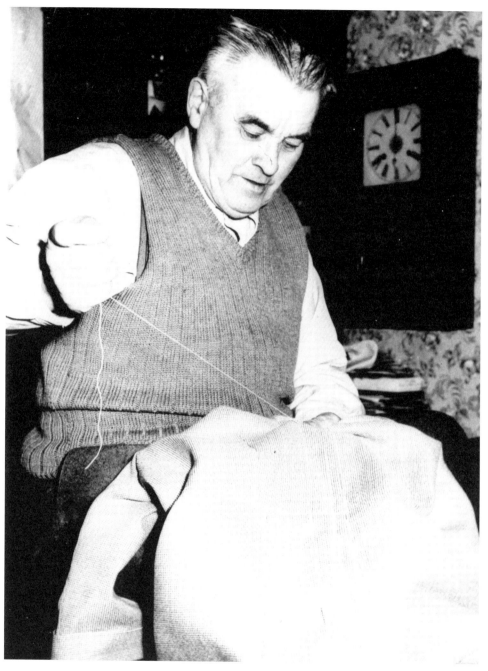

Robert Rowlands at work.

Rowlands with the two Irish Colleens.

Rowlands, working, sitting cross-legged on his table sewing.

accountant, would knock on the Rowlands' front door and run away before the occupants opened it, knowing all too well that Lucy Rowlands, a fiery lady, would blaspheme and shout down Chapel Street at their retreating backs.

Sydney Sandford, 1908–1988

Sydney Sandford was a builder. He joined his father's business after leaving school at the age of fifteen. His father had started the business four years earlier after his demob at the end of the First World War, and had bought ladders, scaffold, barrows and other equipment from another local builder, Jarvis Bewley, with his army gratuity. Their first builders yard was in Llawr Pentre, Old Colwyn, but as they became more successful they moved to a property on Coed Coch Road, eventually ending up at Pendyffryn, Abergele Road, which is now a Grade II listed building. In 1941, now the sole proprietor of the business, Sydney moved his office to Erw Wen Road and lived at Hazel Bank, Seafield Road. Herbert passed on to his son not only his skill but also, more importantly, his care and consideration for a job well done. His style of construction was governed by his instructing architects, chief amongst them Sidney Colwyn Foulkes, and clients, but the finished building was sure evidence of the care and skill that he brought to the job. He built two church houses; St Cynfran's church house at Llysfaen, and the St John's church house on Cliff Road, Old Colwyn, both designed by Sidney Colwyn Foulkes. On Bryn Avenue (on the left as you go up the road), there

St John's church room and theatre, Old Colwyn, built by Sydney Sandford.

are four superb examples of Sydney Sandford's building skills: three houses, No. 5, Brerton, No. 7, South Downs, and No. 25, Windy Ridge, and the nurses' home, which is now an outpatients and physiotherapy department, all built in the 1930s. In 1939, he built Mr Colwyn Foulkes' own home, Moryn, on the corner of Cayley Promenade and Bryn-y-Mor Road in Rhos-on-Sea. Just round the corner (now No. 11 Bryn-y-Mor Road) he built Plas Newydd for Mr Emery, who owned a chain of cinemas in North Wales and Merseyside. Perhaps the best examples of his work are The Wren's Nest on Lansdowne Road and Aldrans on Digby Road; both stand as monuments to an age when a high standard of workmanship and careful construction were important. The style and look of Colwyn Bay is set by architects and planners, but the solidity and permanence of the place rests upon the skill of builders like Sydney Sandford.

Revd William Edwin Sangster, 1900–1960

For the first eight years of his life the Revd Sangster was never taken near a place of worship, but when he was twelve a sensitive teacher asked him if he wanted to become a disciple of Jesus Christ and he honestly replied 'yes'. He became a brilliant preacher and excellent writer, and at the outbreak of the Second World War he was the senior minister of Westminster Central Hall, the 'cathedral' of Methodism. He began his ministry in 1923, at the newly built Rhos-on-Sea Methodist church. He was the first full-time minister of the church. In 1923, he was a young, newly married man, and he had to combine the duties of both St John's English Methodist church, Conwy, and the Rhos church. The two churches were of equal importance and his duties were equally divided. He lived at the Manse in Conway, and bridged the gap between the churches on an ancient bicycle. No church-bound traveller was charged for crossing the toll bridge across the River Conway. In 1927, his children, twins Paul and Margaret, were born. Before the birth, he had told his parishioners that if the child was a girl, he would hoist a pink flag, and if it was a boy, a blue flag. When he discovered that twins had been born, he raised the Union Jack! Paul recalled in later life 'the immense generosity' of the Rhos church in giving £40 'as a church' to help the Revd Sangster with his new babies. In 1929, when the Revd Sangster moved from Rhos-on-Sea to Aintree, two ministers were sent to replace him, one to Conway, and the Revd Fielding to Rhos. In 1940, when he was in London at the Westminster Central Hall, people used to say that on a Sunday morning they would go to The City Temple to hear Revd Dr Leslie Weatherhead because he loved the people, in the afternoon they would listen to Revd Donald Soper at Hyde Park Corner for a good argument, and in the evening they would hear the Revd Sangster because he loved God.

William Edwin Sangster.

Sir Frederick Smith, 1st Baron of Colwyn, PC, Freeman of the Borough of Colwyn Bay, 1859–1946

Lord Colwyn was born in Eccles, and through hard work and diligence became a rubber and cotton manufacturer on a large scale. He was also the deputy chairman of Martin's Bank, a director of several railway companies, and in 1924, he was admitted to the Privy Council. In 1882, he married Elizabeth Anne Savage, who was once described as 'the uncrowned Queen of Colwyn Bay'. They came to live in Colwyn Bay and made their home at Queen's Lodge on Queen's Drive. The huge property was set in the midst of extensive gardens, and they lived there contentedly for the rest of their lives. He was a great benefactor of the town as an active supporter of Colwyn Bay and West Denbighshire Hospital, and he donated the beautiful west window at St Paul's church. The hospital is still in use, and the window still shimmers in the sunlight. On 11 November 1922, it was he who unveiled the new war memorial in front of the town hall on Conwy Road. That town hall has now been demolished, and the memorial has been moved down the road to Queen's Gardens. Lord Colwyn was a popular choice as the charter mayor and he presided over the festivities on 20 September 1934, which were associated with the granting of the Charter to the newly formed Borough of Colwyn Bay. He chaired the ceremony, accompanied the Lord Lt of Denbighshire, Lt-Col. R. W. H. W. Williams-Wynne CB, and then planted a tree in Eirias Park to mark the occasion. The plaque beside the tree is still in place. He was appointed the first official mayor of the Borough of Colwyn Bay in 1935. He died in January 1946, only a few months after the death of his wife.

Lord Colwyn in his motorised wheelchair.

Nell Street MBE, 19 November 1912 – 17 May 2005

In 1957, Maj. Richard Carr-Gorman pioneered the idea of small community houses for the lonely and elderly in Bermondsey. Their first meetings were held in Abbeyfield Road, and it was after this location that the Abbeyfield Society was named. In 1960, the Major contacted Nell Street, without her the Abbeyfield organisation would not exist in Colwyn Bay. It was due to her tireless work over fifty years that the homes were established on Rhos Road (which was eventually knocked down to create an entrance from the road onto the old folks Parkway housing estate), Kenelm Road, Alexandra Road, No. 100 Llanelian Road, Whitehall Road, and the corner of Rhos Road and Allanson Road. She was chairman of the Colwyn Bay Abbeyfield Society for thirty-one years, as well as being an active member of the trustees of Heaton Place Eventide Homes, the National Trust, the Welsh National Opera, the RNLI and the Guide Dogs for the Blind. As was mentioned at her funeral, 'She was interested in everything and everyone; she had an infinite curiosity, but it was not intrusive, because she possessed a genuine sympathy and understanding.' Her father was one of eleven children, ten boys and one girl, and he had worked his way up from the shop floor to become a substantial mill owner. After completing her education in Switzerland, Nell helped him as his secretary and chauffeur. The move to Colwyn Bay was made for the sake of Mr Street's health, but sadly he died only six weeks before his daughter and wife moved into Copley Dene on Ebberston Road West. Nell Street got things done: she was energetic but also practical, when she was invited to become involved in an organisation its goals would quickly and smoothly be realised. She was also a sociable person who enjoyed life to the full and enriched the lives of all those around her.

Suetonius Paulinus, First Century AD

Gaius Suetonius Paulinus was appointed the governor of Britain in AD 59, and two years later he came to Colwyn Bay, marching his 12,000 legionaries along the native tracks and taking a route now marked by Abergele and Conway Roads. He led his men from the present West End of the town to Mochdre, so as to cross the River Conway and slog on to Angelsey, where he intended to put an end to druidism and render the island a useless haven for British fugitives. This was a miscalculation on his part because in the natural defile between Bryn Euryn and the hillside leading up to Bryn Eithin (where today the A55 and the railway line run side by side between the end of Tan-y-Bryn Road and the end of Dinerth Road) he and his troops were ambushed. There was a ferocious battle, and the Romans received an unexpected fright. Suetonius Paulinus' second-in-command, Sempronius, was killed here, and this ravine has since been known as Nant Sempyr. It is also probable that two future governors of Britain, Julius Agricola and Petillius Cerialis, were among Paulinus' legionaries. It may be that the Romans decided not to travel along this dangerous route anymore and that is why they always used the Old Highway from then on. While Suetonius Paulinus was receiving a bloody nose in Colwyn Bay, the tribes of the south-east of Britain, led by Queen Boudica of the Iceni, took the opportunity to stage a revolt, and Suetonius Paulinus had to leave North Wales and hurry back to subdue the unruly Queen and her followers. Thus it was that the feisty folk of the future Colwyn Bay surprised the Romans in battle, but also allowed Queen Boudica to slaughter and torture people in the south of the country.

Nant Sempyr, Brun Euryn on the right, Mochdre through the gap.

Saint Trillo, Born *c.* AD 550

Saint Trillo arrived in what is now Rhos-on-Sea during the reign of Maelgwyn Gwynedd, who had a palace on Bryn Euryn. Saint Trillo was the son of Prince Ithel Hael of Llydaw (The Generous) and the grandson of King Hoel I Maur (The Great), and came to this country from Brittany. He was educated on Bardsey Island to be a saint. In due course he gave his name to the extensive parish of Llandrillo, and he was one of the signatories of the grant that Maelgwyn Gwynedd gave to Saint Kentigern when the see of Bangor was endowed. His fellow signatories were Saint Deiniol, who was the first Bishop of Bangor, Saint Grwst, after whom Llanrwst is named, and Rhun, the son of the King, who gave his name to Caerhun. Saint Trillo has lent his name to the chapel or Cell on the foreshore at Rhos-on-Sea. The chapel is built over a well, and was probably constructed originally to preserve this well, as it is the only one in the neighbourhood. Years ago, the chapel was used by local fishermen where they prayed for success before they put to sea. When Saint Trillo died, his body was taken back to Bardsey Island for burial.

St Trillo's chapel, Rhos-on-Sea.

Revd Lewis Edward Valentine, MA, DD, 1893–1986

Lewis Valentine was born in Llanddulas, where his memorial stands today by the side of the road adjacent to the church. His father was a limestone quarryman who, along with Lewis' grandfather, was a prominent Welsh Calvinistic Methodist minister. After his experiences in the First World War, he met Saunders Lewis and H. R. Jones at the 1925 National Eisteddfod and decided to establish a Welsh political party, the main purpose of which, at that time, was to foster a Welsh-speaking Wales. In 1936, the United Kingdom government agreed that there should be a bombing school at Pen-y-Berth on the Llyn peninsula, and construction began exactly 400 years after the first Act of Union annexing Wales into England. In September 1936, Lewis Valentine, Saunders Lewis and D. J. Williams admitted responsibility for setting fire to the bombing facility. They were found guilty at the Old Bailey and were sentenced to nine months imprisonment in Wormwood Scrubs. On their release they were greeted at the Caernarfon Pavilion by 15,000 Welshmen. During the Second World War, he rejected the idea that the government should force Welshmen to serve in the armed services. He served the church in Colwyn Bay as a pastor, and for twenty-five years edited the Baptist quarterly magazine. He wrote the hymn 'Gweddi dros Gymru' ('A Prayer for Wales'), which is usually sung to the tune of Finlandia composed by Sibelius; some Welshmen consider this hymn as the second Welsh national anthem. In his later years he lived in a flat on Meiriadog Road, Old Colwyn, and then a house on Francis Avenue, Rhos-on-Sea, and when he died his body was cremated at Colwyn Bay Crematorium.

Revd Valentine's memorial in Llanddulas.

Arthur Evelyn St John Waugh, 1903–1966

Evelyn Waugh was one of the great English novelists and the author of *A Handful of Dust*, *Vile Bodies*, *Decline and Fall* and *Brideshead Revisited*. He was a man whom the writer James Lees-Milne asserted was 'the nastiest-tempered man in England', and of whom the critic Clive James wrote, 'Nobody ever wrote a more unaffectedly elegant English … its hundreds of years of steady development culminate in him'. Waugh taught at Arnold House in Llanddulas, and tried to commit suicide by walking into the sea at Llandduals Beach, whereupon he thought better of it when he was attacked by a jellyfish. He was born in London and educated at Heath Mount preparatory school and Lancing College, before going to Hertford College, Oxford. When he was at Heath Mount, he was inclined to bully weaker boys, one of whom was the future photographer Cecil Beaton, who never forgot the experience. After leaving Oxford, he was desperate to earn some money and so applied to an agency for a teaching job, through which he secured the post at Arnold House. The building still stands on Pencoed Road. Mr Waugh found the ambience of the school gloomy, and in truth it still looks rather forbidding. Years later he was to use it as the model for Llanabba Castle in his novel *Decline and Fall*. In the evenings, to avoid the oppressive atmosphere of the school, he would spend a lot of time in the Valentine Pub run by Mrs Roberts, which in *Decline and Fall* he used as the lair of the cretinous Llanabba Silver Band. While at Arnold House, he applied for the job in Pisa as secretary to the Scottish writer Charles Scott Moncrieff. On the assumption that he would get the job, he resigned his position at the school, only to later discover that he had not been successful. While at the school he had also been working on a novel, 'The Temple at Thatch', but had been advised that it was no good. All these disappointments culminated in his attempt to take his life on the Llanddulas beach.

Gordon Scott Whale, 1 April 1893 – 9 January 1966

Gordon Whale was the founder of The Wireless College on East Parade, Colwyn Bay. He learnt his telegraphy in 1912 at the Direct Spanish Telegraph Company, and then in 1916 he was employed by the Marconi Wireless Telegraph Company, first at Connemara and then at Caernarvon. The Marconi Company was installing wireless equipment in British, German, French, Italian and Spanish ships, and at the end of the First World War about 3,000 ships were so equipped. In 1918, Mr Whale realised that there was a market for the training of wireless operators and so, while still an employee of Marconi, he opened a training college at Caernarvon. This venture so infuriated the directors of the Marconi Company that they told him to either close the college or leave the company. He left. In 1920, he moved the college to the White House on Pen-y-Bryn Road, and then in 1923 he moved it again into a former hotel on East Parade. Both the road and the building were demolished to make way for the A55. In 1930, the college expanded into the property next door, and five years later Whale retired to London, leaving his loyal instructors, Charles Oliver and Harry Nelson, to run the college. Five years after his retirement, and after he had opened his second Wireless College in Calmore, Hampshire, he returned to Colwyn Bay, where, because of the Second World War, the East Parade College was busier than ever. In 1944, there were seventy boarding students, five of whom were ladies. Actor Hugh Lloyd was a student at the college, another student went on to be involved in the Apollo space programme, and another became the manager of Goonhilly Satellite Earth Station in Cornwall. Sadly, some of the students lost their lives during the war when the merchant ships on which they were the wireless operators were sunk by German U-boats. After he was demobbed in 1947, Mr Whale's son Neville returned to help his father run the college. The college closed in 1970, and a memorial plaque is now displayed in the car park where the college once stood.

The Wireless College on East Parade, man unknown.

Victor Clarkson Wilde, JP, Freeman of the Borough of Colwyn Bay, 1887–1966

Victor Wilde was a highly respected local landowner, who over many years gave most of the land to the local community. He lived at Odstone, Marine Drive, Rhos-on-Sea, the spot from which it is believed Prince Madog, around 1180, sailed to America. The children's play area at Rhos Point is on land given to the community by Mr Wilde in 1961, in a ceremony presided over by his wife. The plaque at the site, recording this gift, is inscribed with the words: 'To give a little happiness to mothers and children.' He owned the Bryn Euryn Farm at the top end of Rhos Road, which was famous locally for its piggery and the smell that seeped into the surrounding homes. The Marlborough Drive estate below Llandrillo-yn-Rhos parish church was built on his land. The local authority bungalows erected off Elwy Road, on the road christened Victor Wilde Drive, were also built on land that he gave to the Borough Council. When he was presented with the Honorary Freedom of the Borough at Colwyn Bay Civic Centre on 20 April 1966 (on the same occasion that Sidney Colwyn Foulkes also received the same honour), the mayor, Councillor K. B. Jones, said that the honour was bestowed on him as an 'acknowledgement of the distinguished services he has rendered to the Borough of Colwyn Bay by his philanthropic support of many sections of the life of the Borough, of his years of public service as a member of the local authority, of his practical regard over many years for the beauty of the Borough and well-being of its people'. He is buried in Llandrillo-yn-Rhos parish churchyard, beneath a large piece of limestone, on which is inscribed: 'A very good and generous man'.

Bleddyn Llewelyn Williams MBE, 22 February 1923 – 6 July 2009

Bleddyn Williams was a rugby player of instinctive genius, who during the Second World War sensationally flew back from the front line to score a match-winning try for Great Britain. He went on to become the undoubted star of the amateur era immediately after the war. He was known as 'The Prince of Centres', and possessed a natural intelligence and gift of speed and strength, which placed him in a class of his own in the northern hemisphere. The amateur game had given him his real start in life by helping him, in 1936, aged fourteen, to a scholarship at Rydal School in Colwyn Bay, which then had a strong tradition as a rugby nursery. He always remembered the headmaster, the Revd A. J. Costain, once taught him a valuable lesson. Delighted to have beaten four opponents en route to the try line, the Revd Costain took him aside after the game and said, 'If you had passed to your winger, he wouldn't have had to beat anyone'. Mr Williams took the lesson to heart. In his autobiography, he wrote about Revd A. J. Costain: 'From him I learned much. Continually he stressed the necessity for team work … and taught the lessons of unselfish play'. In October 1952, he brought a Cardiff team to Rydal to play a special match against the Rydal Vikings rugby team. The following year, he achieved the distinction of captaining both Cardiff and Wales

So named because Mr Wilde gave the land to the council.

Bleddyn Williams was a giant
of the game in his time.

to victory over the All Blacks in the space of just four days. Mr Williams' close and famous partnership with Jack Matthews, which started in 1942, developed into a close friendship off the field, and Jack Matthews accompanied Mr Williams when he visited Rydal in 2003 to open a new sports hall. At Bleddyn Williams' funeral, Dennis Gethin, president of the Welsh Rugby Union, said of him, 'A man without conceit, a firm believer in fair play and sportsmanship, the values he embodied are timeless.'

John Henry Williams, 29 September 1886 – 7 March 1953

John Henry Williams is the most decorated Welsh NCO of all time. At the start of the First World War, there were so many men wishing to join the army that the training and billeting facilities were overwhelmed. To alleviate the situation, many hundreds of these raw recruits were brought to Colwyn Bay. The first 400 troops to arrive in December 1914, with their commanding officer, Lt-Col. Hamer Greenwood (MP for Sunderland), were the 10th Battalion South Wales Borderers, amongst who was John Henry Williams. They were met at the railway station by the billeting committee, and were billeted in homes between Station Road and the Dingle on the seaward side of Abergele Road, while their commanding officer and his wife lived at Fern Bank, Coed Pella Road. The rate for billeting was, in present day coinage, 17p per day, which was reduced to 15p per day when the number of the troops reached 5,000. For this, the men

Fern Bank, where Williams' commanding officer and his wife were billeted.

were to receive three meals a day, with bacon for breakfast and a cup of tea. Also the householder was to wash one vest, one shirt, one pair of pants and one pair of socks per week! John H. Williams of the 10th South Wales Borderers gained the Distinguished Conduct Medal in July 1916, the Military Medal in July 1917, the bar to the Military Medal in October 1917, and then the Victoria Cross, for action at Villers Outreaux, France, in October 1918. He was wounded and discharged in February 1919, when he received all these decorations at the same investiture from King George V. This was the first time that the King had decorated the same man four times in one day.

Revd W. Venables Williams, MA, Oxon, JP, 29 September 1828 – 9 November 1900

The Revd Venables Williams was the vicar of the parish of Llandrillo-yn-Rhos for thirty-one years (1869–1900). He was a magistrate and chairman of the Colwyn Bay and Colwyn Local Board, which in 1895 became the Colwyn Bay Urban District Council. He won a substantial reduction in the price of education for the poor of the parish, and in 1871 he argued forcibly for the railway to be fully rated at £950 per year. In so doing, he engineered a reduction in local taxes from 5*d* (25p) in the pound to 2/3*d* (11p). When he was first appointed the vicar of Llandrillo-yn-Rhos parish, the parish stretched from Glan Conwy to Eirias Park, which encompassed a population of 900. There was no recognised area of Colwyn Bay. In 1871, in recognition of the emerging importance of the area around Pwllycrochan Halt – later to become Colwyn Bay Railway Station – to the east of Llandrillo church, he started to hold Anglican services in Abel Williams' carpenter's shop in Ivy Street. In 1877, on land donated by Sir Thomas Erskine, he held the first service in a church built on the present site of St Paul's church, which fourteen years later was burnt down by the Mochdre tithe rioters in protest at Revd Venables Williams' condemnation of their unruly behaviour. As a prime mover in its creation, he had anticipated becoming the vicar of the new St Paul's church, as well as of Llandrillo. But with the appointment of a new Bishop of St Asaph, Revd Alfred G. Edwards, a new Colwyn Bay parish was created, and to his bitter disappointment, this post was denied him. There used to be a slate plaque near the railway underpass in Colwyn Bay, which was originally known as 'The Vicar's Road', paying tribute to his foresight in seeing the necessity for this tunnel, while the stretch of Llandudno Road from Llandrillo church to Penrhyn Bay was originally also known as 'The Vicar's Road' because he had been instrumental in acquiring finance for its construction. On the promenade in Rhos-on-Sea, there is a drinking fountain built in 1906 to commemorate his service to the local community.

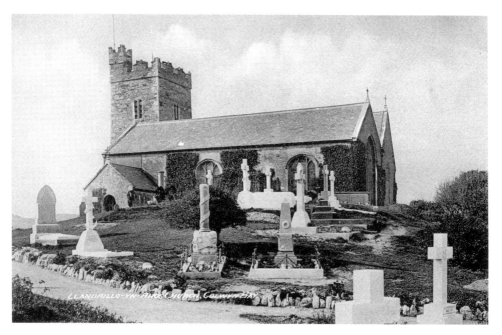

Llandillo's church where the Revd Venables Williams reigned supreme for thirty-one years.

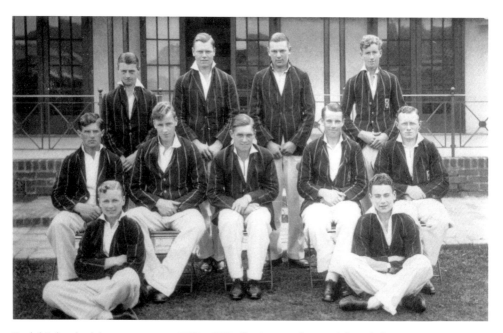

Rydal School cricket team, 1931. Wilfred Wooller is seated second from left.

Wilfred Wooller, 1912–1997

Wilfred Wooller was born at No. 5 Church Road, Rhos-on-Sea. He was the son of the building-business side of the Wooller dynasty, as opposed to the garage-owning side. In later life, he would say that he had been brought up 'as a God-fearing man with a respect for the Establishment'. This was an attitude that got him into a lot of trouble in later life. He went on to be educated at Rydal School, where he first showed his astonishing versatility at all types of games. As a twenty-two-year-old in 1934 and 1935, he played cricket for Denbighshire. After leaving Rydal, he became a renowned Welsh rugby international, and is arguably one of the greatest centre three-quarters of all time: he went on to win eighteen caps, and to captain the Glamorgan side that won the county cricket championship in 1948. He was also a footballer good enough to play for Cardiff City, a squash player for Wales, and an outstanding sprinter. In the 1933 Varsity rugby game, Mr Wooller scored a gigantic drop goal from within his own half. He probably owes his rugby immortality, in Wales and beyond, to a lengthy run that brought about the decisive late score that enabled Wales to beat the 1935/36 All Blacks 13-12 at Cardiff. At the outbreak of the Second World War, he was commissioned into the Royal Artillery. He was captured by the Japanese in Java in 1942 and spent the rest of the war in a POW camp, an experience that may well have exacerbated the brittle forcefulness of his personality. He never suffered fools gladly, and his years with Glamorgan were peppered with controversy; on one occasion he provoked the resignation of half the committee. He was a Test selector from 1955 to 1961, and described Denis Howell, Labour's sports minister, as 'not unlike a 50p piece – double-faced, many-sided and not worth a great deal'. In 1954, at the age of forty-five, he performed the double of scoring 1,000 runs and taking 100 wickets in one season. He was one of the toughest and most successful captains in post-war cricket, and in retirement became the secretary of the club. The umpire Arthur Fagg once came close to throwing a bowl of soup over Mr Wooller. 'I don't care if it costs me my job,' he vowed. 'I'll never umpire Glamorgan again while that man is secretary.'

Mr and Mrs Jones from Plough Terrace.

The Old Colwyn bathing beauty competition in 1947.

*'...for those who lived faithfully a hidden life,
and rest in unvisited tombs'*

John and Margaret Roberts, *c.* 1880 – *c.* 1930

Mr and Mrs Jones kept a fishmongers and fruiterers shop at No. 6 Tai Newyddion, Plough Terrace, Old Colwyn. They travelled around the area in their cart bartering fish and fruit for vegetables and rabbits. Their young daughter, Gertrude, used to be strapped down in a corner of the cart during these journeys.

Gladys Chapman, 1947

Two years after the end of the Second World War, the folk of Old Colwyn reinstated the annual Rose Day, which that year included a Bathing Beauty Competition. The event was won by Gladys Cooper (*née* Chapman), who is the lady on the far right in the picture (opposite page, bottom), standing next to her friend Lal.

Just Passing Through…

Archibald Alexander Leach, 1904–1986

In 1918, young Master Leach, aged fourteen, performed on Colwyn Bay Pier as a member of a troupe of tumblers as part of a traditional English pantomime. He was in Colwyn Bay on the stage of what he later recalled 'a theatre built on, of all windy wintry places, a pier', walking on the second highest stilts in a graduated line of other stilt walkers 'with my head inside a huge papier mâché mask, on which sat a large, white, limp lady's bonnet with a frill around it, and my elongated body and long, long legs encased in a great calico dress'. He later sailed across the Atlantic Ocean, ending up in California and starring in films alongside Frank Sinatra, Leslie Caron, Audrey Hepburn, Grace Kelly and Ingrid Bergman, and changed his name to Cary Grant.

HRH The Prince of Wales, 1894–1972

The future King Edward VIII and Duke of Windsor, accompanied by the local MP Sir Henry Morris Jones, visited Colwyn Bay in 1923. The local dignitaries, including Capt. E. J. Meredith of Meredith & Kirkham Garage, Old Colwyn, were lined up waiting to meet him along the Promenade below the grass embankment between Whitehall Road and Llannerch Road East. A teacher at the Douglas Road Primary School, Louisa Greenfield, told me many years later that she took the children from the school down to the promenade to see the future King. She was somewhat annoyed at the long wait, with the pupils becoming ever more restless, until the Prince eventually arrived over an hour late. It was rumoured, and Miss Greenfield testified to me, that it was obvious by his appearance that he had enjoyed himself too much at his last luncheon stop in Llandudno. Miss Greenfield had to stop teaching because she became a married woman, marrying Mr Cheadle.

Where Cary Grant performed in 1918.

David Ivor (Novello) Davies, 1893–1951

Ivor Novello's mother was Madame Clara Novello Davies, an internationally recognised singing teacher and choral conductor, who lived for a time in Colwyn Bay, where her son would often visit her. She doted on her son and he adopted her maiden name as his stage name. In 1914, he wrote the patriotic wartime song 'Keep the Home Fires Burning', which was sung on many occasions at the Pier Pavilion in Colwyn Bay. Madame Davies enjoyed her time in Colwyn Bay, where she stayed with friends in Rhos-on-Sea while she gave private singing lessons at a private school opposite Colwyn Bay Hotel. Her son admitted that without his mother's help and encouragement, he would not have had the successes that came his way, and so made time to visit Colwyn Bay on numerous occasions to see his maternal mentor. John Stuart Roberts, Siegfried Sassoon's biographer, wrote of Ivor that he 'was a consummate flirt who collected lovers as he gathered lilacs'. It is not recorded as to whether he gathered any lilacs in the traditional Colwyn Bay.

Frank Lincoln Wright, 1867–1959

After his unreliable father left home and divorced his mother, Anna Lloyd Jones, Frank dropped his middle name and adopted his mother's middle name. In due course, he became the man the American Institute of Architects called 'the greatest American architect of all time'. His mother was a school teacher whose parents, Richard and

Frank Lloyd Wright, Ralph Colwyn Foulkes and Clough Williams-Ellis in the garden of Cotswold, *c.* 1954.

Mary Jones, had emigrated from Taliesin, a Welsh village near Llandysul, Cardiganshire. Frank Lloyd Wright designed 1,000 structures, and also designed the furniture, the carpets and the stained glass windows for many of his buildings. One of his houses, Fallingwater, has been called 'the best all-time work of American architecture'. The Imperial Hotel in Tokyo, which he designed in 1923, survived the earthquake of the same year, and the American bombs of the Second World War. He was a friend of Clough Williams-Ellis, the creator of Port Meirion, and in 1956 came to stay with him, and to receive an Honorary Doctorate from the University of Wales at a ceremony at Bangor University. One morning, unannounced, Clough Williams-Ellis brought his friend to see Sidney Colwyn Foulkes in Colwyn Bay. Mr Colwyn Foulkes and his son Ralph showed the great American architect around his studio, his home, Cotswold, on Brackley Avenue, and his Japanese garden in the grounds of Cotswold. Four of them then also went on a tour of the Maes Glas-Bryn Eglwys Estate in Rhos-on-Sea, designed by Mr Colwyn Foulkes. While he was in North Wales, he went missing and was later discovered in a taxi heading for Taliesin – the village where his beloved mother and her family had originated and after which he named both his homes in the United States of America. Had he known, it would have been easier for him to have taken a taxi to Llyn Geirionydd where there is a monument at the head of the lake commemorating the belief that this was where Taliesin was born and was buried.

Bibliography

Bevan, Frances, *A Year's March Nearer Heaven* (Privately printed by the author, 2009)

Bott, Caroline G., *The Life & Works of Alfred Bestall, Illustrator of Rupert Bear* (Bloomsbury, 2011)

Deacon, Richard, *Madoc & the Discovery of America, 1170* (New York, 1965)

Denison, Simon, *Welsh Fort Identified as Citidal of Dark Age King* (*British Archaeology*, Issue 29, 1997)

Draper, Christopher and John Lawson-Reay, *Scandal at Congo Institute* (Gwasg Carreg Gwalch, 2012)

Edwards, Geoffrey, *The Borough of Colwyn Bay – A Social History 1934–1974* (Colwyn Borough Council, 1984)

Eyles, Allen, *Odeon Cinemas: Oscar Deutsch Entertains Our Nation* (Cinema Theatre Association, 2002)

Foulkes, A. D. D., *Colwyn Bay in 1868: A Chatty Survey with Many Subsequent Recollections* (Arthur Dunwell, 1935)

Grant, Mairwena, *Meirion Roberts – The Public Image* (Clwyd Library & Information Service, 1995, monograph accompanying an exhibition)

Guy, Marjorie May, *Joe Doughty* (A & C Black, 1918)

Hammond, John Lang, *Through North Wales, Being an Account of Some Walks, Tours and Climbs in that Country* (Privately written, never published, 1938)

Hignell, Andrew, *The Skipper: A Biography of Wilf Wooller* (Limlow Books, 1995)

Hovey, Rosa, *Penrhos 1880–1930* (Printed by the school, 1930)

Hughes, John, *Briwsion Bro – A Book about the Llangernyw/Llanfair TH Community* (Privately printed, 1986)

Jones, Marian Giles, *Missionary in Manitoba: The Papers of Isaiah Brookes-Jones 1884-1907* (Denbigh: Gee & Sons, *c.* 1965)

Noble, Peter, *Ivor Novello* (The Falcon Press, 1951)

Owen, Robert and John Gruffydd Owen, *Darlum O Arlunydd, E Meirion Roberts* (Caernarfon: Wasg Gwynedd, 1995)

Roberts, Eunice and Helen Morley, *The Spirit of Colwyn Bay 1 & 2* (Landmark Publishing, 2002)

Roberts, Graham, *Colwyn Bay Through Time* (Amberley Publishing, 2009)

Roberts, Graham, *Colwyn Bay at War* (Amberley Publishing, 2012)

Roberts, Graham, 'Frank Lloyd Wright', *Colwyn Bay Civic Society Journal* (Colwyn Bay Civic Society, March 2001)

Roberts, Graham, *Colwyn Bay & District: a Collection of Pictures*, Volumes 1–3 (Bridge Books)

Roberts, W. Arvon, *Famous Welsh Americans* (Pwllheli: Llygad Gwalch, 2008)

Sangster, Elizabeth, *W. E. S. A Daughter's Tribute* (Epworth Press, 1961)

Sarkar, Dilip, *Spitfire Voices* (Amberley, 2010)

Thomas, Dilys, *Memories of Old Colwyn* (Bridge Books, 2000)

Timothy, Revd T. E., *Llandrillo-yn-Rhos* (Shrewsbury: L. Wilding, 1910)

Tucker, Norman, *Colwyn Bay Its Origin and Growth* (Colwyn Borough Council, 1953)

Tynan Kathleen, *The Life of Kenneth Tynan* (Weidenfeld & Nicolson, 1987)

Venables-Williams, Revd W., *An Archaeological History of Llandrillo-yn-Rhos & Immediate Neighbourhood* (R. E. Jones & Bros, 1890)

Voeleker, Adam, *Herbert Luck North* (Royal Commission of the Ancient Monuments of Wales, 2013)

Watkinson, Peter, *The Osborns & Rydal Mount School 1885–1919* (Rydal Penrhos School, 2004)

Acknowledgements

Miss Sonia Ankers, Mike Breese, David Coathup, Aline Davies (*née* Firth), the late Hilda Frankland (the adopted child of Ellen Madren), Norman Hood, Michael Hovey, Nick Jackson, Paul Raynor, Jennifer Roberts, Chris Somerville, the late Dilys Thomas, and Neville Whale.

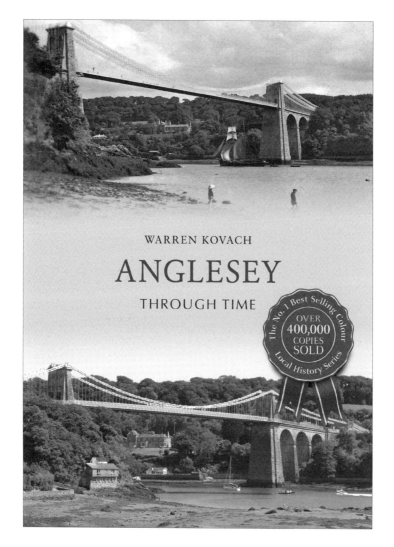

Anglesey Through Time

Warren Kovach

This fascinating selection of photographs traces some of the many ways in which Anglesey has changed and developed over the last century.

978 1 4456 1652 0
96 pages, full colour

Available from all good bookshops or order direct from our website www.amberleybooks.com

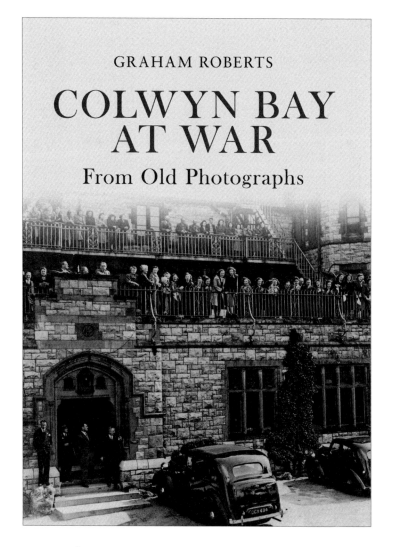

Paranormal Anglesey

Bunty Austin

A fascinating tour of ghostly encounters from the haunted hub of
North Wales.

978 1 84868 315 0
128 pages, illustrated throughout